"There is no passage of Scripture I have turned to as frequently or as desperately as Psalm 23. It has blessed, guided, and strengthened me in my hardest seasons and darkest days. Yet I have not come close to mastering its content or exhausting its riches—something that became clear as I read this lovely, helpful, challenging, easy-to-read guide to one of the Bible's brightest treasures. I give it my highest recommendation."

Tim Challies, author, *Seasons of Sorrow*

"To read this book is to sit under the best pastoral care—that of a pastor who expounds God's word clearly, lovingly, and with delight. The word shines here, as we take time to follow the whole shape of Psalm 23; ultimately, the Savior of the Scriptures shines, Jesus the good shepherd, who is with us all the way home."

Kathleen Nielson, author; speaker

"*The Lord of Psalm 23* combines an attentive reading of the text with rich theological insight, all brought together to nourish and comfort the heart. I warmly encourage you to read it and meet the Lord afresh. This book was a tonic for my own soul at a time when I was feeling overwhelmed."

Tim Chester, Senior Faculty Member, Crosslands Training

"Reading Psalm 23 through the lens of union with Christ—the good shepherd incarnate—*The Lord of Psalm 23* brings assurance, comfort, and guidance to those of us who ask, 'Can the Lord prepare a table in the wilderness?' This is a wonderful encouragement."

Michael Horton, J. Gresham Machen Professor of Systematic Theology and Apologetics, Westminster Seminary California

"A pastor's heart breathes through this book. Just as the psalm's own words are heartwarming and beautiful, so on the lips of a caring pastor these meditations warm the heart and delight the soul. They did me good. They will do you good."

Christopher Ash, Writer in Residence, Tyndale House, Cambridge

"There are two ways of reading and studying Scripture. One is like clipping down a motorway, traversing big chunks, getting the sweep of the story. The other is like milking a cow—you just sit there with one text and keep pulling and squeezing. The latter is what David Gibson does with Psalm 23—he 'milks' it marvelously, and your cup will run over!"

Dale Ralph Davis, former pastor; Former Professor of Old Testament, Reformed Theological Seminary, Jackson

"The Psalter is the hymnbook of the Bible. God's people were instructed to come into his presence with singing and into his courts with praise (Ps. 100:2, 4). As they lifted up their hearts in song, they gave voice to their laments and tears as well. No psalm is likely more beloved and consequently more abused than the twenty-third. In this short book, David Gibson unpacks the beauty and depth behind these almost too familiar words so we can hear and sing them anew."

Harold Senkbeil, Executive Director Emeritus, DOXOLOGY: The Lutheran Center for Spiritual Care and Counsel

"An old text has become a new friend. After reading *The Lord of Psalm 23*, I have fallen in love with this psalm all over again. David Gibson draws out its blessings with profound and soul-stirring richness. As you read this little volume, the beauty of the good shepherd will shine with even greater brightness in your mind's eye. What a great shepherd, companion, and host we have in Jesus; and this book brings that truth to full light. Read it, meditate on it, and pray over it. Doing so is time well spent, because it is time spent taking in the glories of Christ."

Jason Helopoulos, Senior Pastor, University Reformed Church, East Lansing, Michigan

"*The Lord of Psalm 23* is a superbly well-titled and rare gem of pastoral theology. David Gibson demonstrates great skill in shining fresh light on the familiar verses, with delightful felicity of expression, fueled by penetrating, insightful reflection. Widely researched, with detailed attention to the text, and rooted in practical application, the book fills our vision with the shepherd Lord himself and brings us to worship him in renewed amazement and appreciation of his covenant grace and mercy. Reading this sensitive and warmhearted pastoral exposition has been a refreshing spiritual tonic to my soul."

David Jackman, Former President, The Proclamation Trust

"Just when you thought you knew all there was to know of Psalm 23, along comes David Gibson's deep and pastoral dive into this beautiful psalm. Your mind will be sharpened and your heart warmed as the author walks you through each verse with precision and a pastor's eye. And with every step, he points us to Jesus, the true good shepherd, who came to lead us home. I loved it!"

Jenny Salt, Associate to Archdeacon Women's Ministry, Sydney Anglican Diocese; Host, *Salt—Conversations with Jenny*

"The beauty of David Gibson's journey through the Twenty-Third Psalm is its sustained focus on God. When the Lord is your shepherd, you have everything you need. His wisdom will lead you. His rest will restore you. His presence is with you. His strength will protect you. And his goodness and mercy will follow you all the way home. Read this book, and your soul will be nourished with a fresh view of all that is yours in Christ."

Colin Smith, Senior Pastor, The Orchard, Arlington Heights, Illinois; Founder and Bible Teacher, *Open the Bible*

The Lord of Psalm 23

Other Crossway Books by David Gibson

Living Life Backward: How Ecclesiastes Teaches Us to Live in Light of the End

Radically Whole: Gospel Healing for the Divided Heart

From Heaven He Came and Sought Her: Definite Atonement in Historical, Biblical, Theological, and Pastoral Perspective, edited with Jonathan Gibson

The Lord of Psalm 23

Jesus Our Shepherd, Companion, and Host

David Gibson

Foreword by Sinclair B. Ferguson

CROSSWAY®

WHEATON, ILLINOIS

The Lord of Psalm 23: Jesus Our Shepherd, Companion, and Host
Copyright © 2023 by David Gibson
Published by Crossway
    1300 Crescent Street
    Wheaton, Illinois 60187

Cover design: Jordan Singer

First printing 2023

Printed in China

Hardcover ISBN: 978-1-4335-8798-6
ePub ISBN: 978-1-4335-8801-3
PDF ISBN: 978-1-4335-8799-3

Library of Congress Cataloging-in-Publication Data

Names: Gibson, David, 1975– author. | Ferguson, Sinclair B., writer of foreword.
Title: The Lord of Psalm 23 : Jesus our Shepherd, companion, and host / David Gibson ; foreword by Sinclair B. Ferguson.
Other titles: Lord of Psalm twenty three
Description: Wheaton, Illinois : Crossway, 2023. | Includes bibliographical references and index.
Identifiers: LCCN 2022058467 (print) | LCCN 2022058468 (ebook) | ISBN 9781433587986 (hardcover) | ISBN 9781433587993 (pdf) | ISBN 9781433588013 (epub)
Subjects: LCSH: Bible. Psalms, XXIII—Commentaries.
Classification: LCC BS1450 23rd .G48 2023 (print) | LCC BS1450 23rd (ebook) | DDC 223/.207—dc23/eng/20230321
LC record available at https://lccn.loc.gov/2022058467
LC ebook record available at https://lccn.loc.gov/2022058468

Crossway is a publishing ministry of Good News Publishers.

RRD   34   33   32   31   30   29   28   27   26   25   24
14   13   12   11   10   9   8   7   6   5   4   3   2

For Drew Tulloch

*In Him I have an offering, an altar, a temple, a priest,
a sun, a shield, a Savior, a Shepherd, a hiding place,
a resting place, food, medicine, riches, honor, wisdom,
righteousness, holiness, in short, everything.*

JOHN NEWTON

Contents

Foreword

OCCASIONALLY IN THE CHAPEL SERVICES at the seminary where I taught, one of the students would introduce the guest preacher with the four magical words "He is my minister." There are few descriptions under-shepherds of Christ's flock value more than these simple words expressing the special bond of affection that exists between pastor and people. I have never had the opportunity to use these words—that is, until now. For David Gibson is not only my friend; he is my minister. By the time you have finished reading these pages, you will realize why I count it a great privilege to sit under his ministry.

The Lord of Psalm 23 takes us through the six verses of what—at least where I come from—is by far the best-known and most frequently sung psalm in the Bible. In the days when hymnbooks were standard issue in churches, in many places—not least, funeral chapels—the books almost opened themselves at Psalm 23. I have known that psalm almost since I learned to talk, or at least since a well-meaning aunt gave me a child's storybook version of it as a present. Its words (especially sung to the tune "Crimond") have been the soundtrack of my life. It is not entirely my aunt's fault, however, that I have not always appreciated it. Where her kind gift misled me was the way its front cover pictured David, the psalmist. There he sits beside a rock, a young teenager with glowing complexion, handsome face, spotless clothes, and an untarnished shepherd's crook. This David was exactly the kind of boy I was not and never would be. Familiarity with this image did not so much breed contempt as cloud my mind to what generations of believers had found life-sustaining and soul-nourishing in this great psalm.

I suspect others share my experience. I cannot now recall exactly when all this changed; but I know what caused the change and opened my eyes to the obvious truth that lies on the surface of the text. What was needed was to experience some degree of what David describes in verse 4 as deep darkness, "the valley of the shadow of death." Then the ghost of my childhood image of the psalmist would be exorcised. Then it would become clear that this psalm is not the product of an untried shepherd boy musing on how God is like him but the testimony of someone who bears the scars of trials, failures, loss, and—yes—the sins of his youth that led him two psalms later to ask God not to remember them (Ps. 25:7). This David had been in the valley of deep darkness; he had tasted the supplies of God even when—indeed, especially when—surrounded by his enemies. It was then he had learned what his forefather Jacob meant when he spoke of the Lord as "the God who has been my shepherd all my life long" (Gen. 48:15).

Probably you are holding this book in your hands because you wonder (as I did) *why* this psalm has meant so much to so many Christians, or because it has meant so much to you personally, and you are eager to discover more of its riches. In either case, you are putting your hands—and more importantly your mind and heart—into the safe hands of David Gibson. His ministry combines the quality of intellect and insight that makes him an outstanding expositor of Scripture (more able than he himself realizes) with the heart and devotion of a pastor who loves the church he serves. Here, in *The Lord of Psalm 23*, he shares with all of us the food that has first nourished his own flock. And if I say that the content of this book is typical of the quality of his ministry (not just an unusual "spike" in it), I hope this will reassure you of the integrity and reliability of what he writes here. I feel sure that, like many others who have told me how much they have valued David Gibson's other books, you will want to read more from him in the future. But, first, you are about to appreciate and enjoy this one!

Sinclair B. Ferguson

A Note on Singing the Twenty-Third Psalm

PSALM 23 IS A SUPERLATIVE SONG of confident trust in God. Its words of praise radiate with delight in the Lord as they cause us to worship him for who he is and what he does. The poetic beauty of its heartfelt adoration means, of course, that there are as many different versions of the Twenty-Third Psalm in hymns and songs as there are interpretations of it in commentaries, sermons, and other theological tomes.

This book originated in a series of three sermons preached to the Trinity Church family in Aberdeen, and in our worship services we followed each sermon by singing a different version of the psalm. These are included at the ends of the three parts of this book.

The first hymn, written by Christopher Idle in 1977, is "The Lord My Shepherd Rules My Life." Idle wrote it, he said, "to provide a version of the twenty-third Psalm in familiar meter which would avoid the archaism and inversions of the established sixteenth-century version of the Scottish Psalter." He sought to capture the biblical view of a shepherd, whose role is to rule rather than coddle and cosset his sheep. His choice of tune, "Brother James' Air," was composed by James Leith Macbeth Bain (ca. 1840–1925), who was born in Perthshire, Scotland. Bain was a healer, mystic, and poet known to his friends as Brother James. The tune is twelve bars long and so requires the last two lines of each verse to be repeated.

Next is a hymn from the 1650 Scottish Psalter, "The Lord's My Shepherd, I'll Not Want." This is probably the best known of all metrical versions of the Psalms. The text was written by the English Puritan William Whittingham (1524–1579), a translator of the Geneva Bible who married John Calvin's sister and succeeded John Knox as pastor of the English-speaking congregation in Geneva. Whittingham was dean of Durham from 1563 until his death. The hymn is in common meter, and so, many tunes fit its text. In recent years, however, the tune "Crimond" has become the favorite, with "Wiltshire" a close second. "Crimond" was composed by Jessie Seymour Irvine, whose father was at one time minister in the village of Crimond in Aberdeenshire. Queen Elizabeth heard the tune at Crathie Church, where the royal family worships when staying at Balmoral Castle. She chose it for her wedding in Westminster Abbey in 1947, and it was sung there again at her state funeral in 2022 as the second Elizabethan age drew to a close.

The third version included here is my favorite, "The King of Love My Shepherd Is." This paraphrase was penned by Henry Williams Baker (1821–1877), a vicar in the Anglican Church. He was editor in chief of the iconic hymnbook *Hymns Ancient and Modern*, for which he wrote a number of texts. John Bacchus Dykes was music editor for the hymnary, and he wrote the beautiful tune *"Dominus regit me"* specifically (the opening phrase of the psalm in Latin). The Irish tune "St Columba" is found in some hymnals and suits the text very well. The hymn has six verses corresponding to the six verses of the psalm. There is New Testament imagery: the "ransom" is from Matthew 20:28, and the "living water" from John 4:10; and the fourth verse says, "Your cross before to guide me." There are other rich allusions to the Lord Jesus in this hymn, which we will come to later in the book.

The choice of these songs over others does nothing to denigrate the many alternative renderings of Psalm 23 set to music and verse. Rather, these are presented here simply to aid your worship as you read this book and to add yet more layers—an idea you will encounter a lot in this exposition—to the treasures contained in the psalm.

The combination of words of address in sermon and words of response in song and prayer is part of the powerful rhythm of corporate worship. It enables us to perceive the same reality from different angles and to engage the reality of who God is with all our being. May the words of these hymns and the words of this book combine to move your heart, soul, mind, and strength to love Christ more.

The theologian and the hymn writer traverse day by day the same country, the Kingdom of our Lord. They walk the same paths; they see the same objects; but in their methods of observation and their reports of what they see they differ. So far as theology is a science the theologian deals simply with the topography of the country; he explores, he measures, he expounds. So far as hymn writing is an art the writer deals not with the topography but with the landscape: he sees, he feels, and he sings. The difference in method is made inevitable by the variance of temperament of the two men, the diversity of gifts. But both methods are as valuable as inevitable. Neither man is sufficient in himself either as an observer or a reporter. It is the topography and the landscape together that make the country what it is. It is didactics and poetry together that can approach the reality of the spiritual kingdom.[1]

1   Louis F. Benson, *The Hymnody of the Christian Church* (Richmond, VA: John Knox, 1956), 25.

The Twenty-Third Psalm

A PSALM OF DAVID

The LORD is my shepherd; I shall not want.
    He makes me lie down in green pastures.
He leads me beside still waters.[1]
    He restores my soul.
He leads me in paths of righteousness[2]
    for his name's sake.

Even though I walk through the valley of the shadow of
      death,[3]
    I will fear no evil,
for you are with me;
    your rod and your staff,
    they comfort me.

---

1 Hebrew *beside waters of rest.*
2 Or *in right paths.*
3 Or *the valley of deep darkness.*

You prepare a table before me
     in the presence of my enemies;
you anoint my head with oil;
     my cup overflows.
Surely[4] goodness and mercy[5] shall follow me
     all the days of my life,
and I shall dwell[6] in the house of the LORD
     forever.[7]

4   Or *Only.*
5   Or *steadfast love.*
6   Or *shall return to dwell.*
7   Hebrew *for length of days.*

Introduction

SOME TEXTS OF HOLY SCRIPTURE are hard to preach on or write about, not because they are especially difficult for the pastor or theologian to understand but because they are already so profoundly precious to the hearer and reader.

I suspect this is more true of Psalm 23 than of any other part of the Bible.

I came to preach on this psalm to my own church family after visiting a dear friend in the congregation who was hospitalized for major, life-changing surgery. After his operation, for several weeks my friend was able to read only very small portions of text. One day he showed me his copy of W. Phillip Keller's book *A Shepherd Looks at Psalm 23*. Keller reads the individual phrases of the psalm through his shepherd eyes and runs each word through his shepherd hands; the result is a thoughtful and intimate reading of Psalm 23.[1] We discussed the book and why it was helpful, and as I walked home that day, the idea for three sermons on Psalm 23 came to me. I did some reading and initial study, outlined the sermon series in a way

---

1   W. Phillip Keller, *A Shepherd Looks at Psalm 23* (Grand Rapids, MI: Zondervan, 1970).

that seemed to make sense, and even sourced a picture of a deep, dark valley to advertise the sermon series to our congregation. It was sure to whet their appetite! I proudly showed my artwork to my friend next time I visited the hospital.

"No," he said, almost immediately. "That hillside in your picture is so soft and gentle you could do forward rolls all the way down! In my mind 'the valley of the shadow of death' looks and feels like the valley in *The Pilgrim's Progress*."

We will come to that valley later in this book, and to John Bunyan's vivid depiction of it. Bunyan certainly helped me understand it much better, and I hope I can do it justice here. But my friend revealed something that might happen as you read these pages. Psalm 23 has comforted so many of us during the most painful and difficult moments of our lives that to have someone else analyze it line by line and tell you what it means, when you have already felt what it means in such a precious way, can be a profoundly disappointing experience. If you've actually lived in the valley, you don't need me trying to describe it to you. That feels like taking something beautifully well-worn and exquisitely comfortable out of your hands, playing around with it, knocking it out of shape, and handing it back to you now beyond recognition.

I hope and pray your experience will not be like this. My aim is for this exposition to be like revisiting an old friend, with the familiarity and ease of such an encounter offering a gateway to learning new and unexpected things that detract in no way from what the two of you already have but, rather, serve only to add new layers of depth.

The riches in this psalm are inexhaustible. We will see that even the small phrases in it are, to use Martin Luther's lovely phrase, "a little Bible."[2] These six short verses are a window into the sixty-six books of Scripture, and they take us through the whole story of redemption in an elevated, majestic, and also personal, intimate way. In the pages that follow, I simply want to walk through each phrase of the psalm and, as best I can, portray the beauty of its meaning for us. The walk will not be linear, like a straight line tracing the tightly composed argument of an epistle. Rather, this journey will be more circuitous and involve revisiting some parts of the psalm in light of its other parts and, indeed, other portions of the Bible.

On the one hand, "this Psalm is so clear, that there is no real need to comment upon it";[3] on the other hand, it contains numerous words and ideas that are "open ended" and regularly "under defined."[4] I trust that in what you read here you won't lose track of that first truth about the clarity of Psalm 23, and that your experience of the Lord Jesus as shepherd will only become richer and sweeter. That goal can also be realized because of the second truth about the "open ended" nature of the psalm. This reality is not to be feared. You will see that the English Standard Version, which I am working with in this book, and which is printed in full at the start, contains no less than seven footnotes on issues of translation, and we will engage with many matters like this. So, simply by reading this version of the psalm, we are already embarking on a path of finding more treasures in this psalm than meet the eye on a first reading. This combination of truths about

2 Cited in William S. Plumer, *Psalms: A Critical and Expository Commentary with Doctrinal and Practical Remarks* (Edinburgh: Banner of Truth, 1975), 7.

3 David Firth, *Hear, O Lord: A Spirituality of the Psalms* (Calver, UK: Cliff College Publishing, 2005), 36, cited in Richard S. Briggs, *The Lord Is My Shepherd: Psalm 23 for the Life of the Church* (Grand Rapids, MI: Baker Academic, 2021), 65.

4 Briggs, *The Lord Is My Shepherd*, 66, 99.

Psalm 23 is part of why the psalm is universally loved and also why we will not quickly plumb all the depths it contains.

I am going to lead us through Psalm 23 with the help of Alec Motyer's incisive outline, which is tucked away, almost obscurely, in *The New Bible Commentary*. Out of gratitude for his outstanding work as a commentator, I have retrieved Motyer's profile of the psalm, and it has guided my reading here in three vignettes: the sheep and the shepherd (vv. 1–3), the traveler and the companion (v. 4), and the guest and the host (vv. 5–6). As part of this, Motyer observes that each of these sections has a personal confession at its heart—"I shall not want" (v. 1), "I shall not fear" (v. 4), and "I shall dwell" (v. 6)—with the reason for these three confident assertions beautifully explained in each section.[5]

If these portions of the psalm make up its skeletal structure, then the spine of the psalm is the close, deeply personal relationship between its author and the person it describes. This is expressed as a "he-me" relationship in the opening lines, which is close enough, but then most beautifully and seamlessly becomes "you-me" in the valley of the shadow of death. As Motyer says, "The darker the shadow, the closer the Lord!"[6] From that point on, the psalm only ever directly addresses the Lord as good shepherd, closest companion, and generous host.

This means that this psalm is in our Bibles as an exquisite depiction of the Lord Jesus Christ. More than that, it is a song of personal praise flowing from what it means to know and adore

---

5 Alec Motyer, *New Bible Commentary* (Leicester, UK: Inter-Varsity Press, 1994), 500. So too Susan Gillingham, *Psalms through the Centuries: A Reception History Commentary on Psalms 1–72*, vol. 2 (West Sussex, UK: Wiley Blackwell, 2018), 145.

6 Motyer, *New Bible Commentary*, 500.

him as belonging to *me*, personally. So in these pages, in faltering words, I have one simple aim: to show you in the images, poetic beauty, and themes of Psalm 23 just how the Lord Jesus takes complete and absolute responsibility for those who are in his care.

I believe this is the point of the shepherding imagery, which blends into the hosting imagery. In the ancient Near East, shepherds were entirely and absolutely responsible for their sheep, and hosts were entirely and absolutely responsible for their guests.[7] This is why the words of this psalm have nourished God's people ever since they were written down. From start to end, the language describing God is active, intensive, causative—he *makes*, he *leads*, he *restores*, he *leads* again, he is *with* me, he *prepares*, he *anoints*. Through the doorway of only six short verses, we enter a world of the most stunning beauty because of whom we meet once inside the psalm and because of what he does for us as we walk through life with him. Psalm 23 teaches that if we belong to Christ, we are in a world of active initiative, of strength, of leadership and protection; it is a relationship of the very best and most secure intentional care.[8]

Throughout church history many of our best-loved theologians and pastors have seen that what Jesus offers us is so comprehensive precisely because what he gives us is himself. He gives us everything we need because he himself is everything we need. The scale of his sufficiency has drawn forth some of the most beautiful lines we have in Christian theology. Consider, for example, John Calvin's depiction of all that Jesus is for us, both in his person and in the work he accomplishes:

7   I owe this point to my brother Jonathan Gibson in "Comfort for All of Life," a sermon on Ps. 23 preached at Cambridge Presbyterian Church, February 28, 2016, https://www.cambridgepres.org.uk/.

8   Gibson, "Comfort for All of Life."

We see that our whole salvation and all its parts are comprehended in Christ. . . . If we seek strength, it lies in his dominion; if purity, in his conception; if gentleness, it appears in his birth. . . . If we seek redemption, it lies in his passion; if acquittal, in his condemnation; if remission of the curse, in his cross; if satisfaction, in his sacrifice; if purification, in his blood; if reconciliation, in his descent into hell; if mortification of the flesh, in his tomb; if newness of life, in his resurrection; if immortality, in the same; if inheritance of the Heavenly Kingdom, in his entrance into heaven; if protection, if security, if abundant supply of all blessings, in his Kingdom; if untroubled expectation of judgment, in the power given to him to judge. In short, since rich store of every kind of good abounds in him, let us drink our fill from this fountain, and from no other.[9]

Calvin's words reach these eloquent heights because of his profound grasp of the doctrine of union with Christ—all that is Christ's becomes ours through our faith-union with him.

Although the grammar of Psalm 23 is different from this, I want to show you that the theological worldview of Psalm 23 is not. Indeed, it is in the imagery of the psalm (sheep with a shepherd, traveler with a companion, guest with a host) that we see the tangible, pictorial resonances of union with our Savior. Your being united to Christ is not a doctrine floating somewhere out there in the abstract theological ether, nor is it confined to the pages of dusty systematic theologies. Rather, it is the very essence of what it means to be a Christian and

---

9   John Calvin, *Institutes of the Christian Religion*, ed. John T. McNeill, trans. Ford Lewis Battles (Philadelphia: Westminster, 1960), 2.16.19.

to have the Lord Jesus as *your* shepherd. You belong to him—completely, absolutely—and because of who he is, you have everything you need.

My simple prayer for this book, in the words of William Gadsby's hymn of praise to the Lord Jesus, is that through its pages your "soul could love and praise him more."

Immortal honours rest on Jesus' head,
my God, my portion and my living bread;
in him I live, upon him cast my care;
he saves from death, destruction and despair.

He is my refuge in each deep distress,
the Lord my strength and glorious righteousness;
through floods and flames he leads me safely on
and daily makes his sovereign goodness known.

My every need he richly will supply,
nor will his mercy ever let me die;
in him there dwells a treasure all divine
and matchless grace has made that treasure mine.

O that my soul could love and praise him more,
his beauties trace, his majesty adore,
live near his heart, rest in his love each day,
hear his dear voice and all his will obey.[10]

---

10 Words by William Gadsby © in this version Praise Trust / www.praise.org.uk. Used by permission.

PART 1

THE SHEEP AND
THE SHEPHERD

The LORD is my shepherd; I shall not want.
He makes me lie down in green pastures.
He leads me beside still waters.
He restores my soul.
He leads me in paths of righteousness
for his name's sake.

PSALM 23:1–3

CHARLES SPURGEON CALLED Psalm 23 "the pearl of the Psalms."[1] We all know why.

Those who know and love the Lord Jesus find that this psalm's "soft and pure radiance delights every eye. . . . Its piety and its poetry are equal, its sweetness and its spirituality are unsurpassed."[2] In different versions of the Bible, through varied versions in songs and hymns, the words of Psalm 23 are embedded in the collective consciousness of the Christian church the world over. Athanasius said, "Most of Scripture speaks *to* us; the Psalms speak *for* us."[3] If the psalms are precious, speaking the language of the heart's personal experience of God, Psalm 23 is the pearl because it combines a beautiful picture of who God is with a beautiful picture of what God does, and it does so all the while simply assuming that this marriage of divine person and heavenly benefits is the personal experience of every believer: "The LORD is *my* shepherd" (v. 1).

In part 1 of this book we will consider the first three verses of Psalm 23. We are going to see three beautiful things about our shepherd: who he is, what he provides, and where he leads.

---

1   Charles Spurgeon, *The Treasury of David*, 3 vols. (Peabody, MA: Hendrickson, 1988), 1:351.

2   Spurgeon, *The Treasury of David*, 1:351.

3   Athanasius, *Letter to Marcellinus*, paraphrased in John Goldingay, *Psalms*, vol. 1, *Psalms 1–41* (Grand Rapids, MI: Baker Academic, 2006), 23 (emphasis added).

1

Who He Is

MANY READERS, COMMENTATORS, and preachers move so quickly to the main imagery of Psalm 23—sheep and shepherd, pastures and water, and the poetic lilt of the valley of the shadow of death—that they, and we, don't pause at the stunning beauty of the opening phrase.

There are only four Hebrew words in Psalm 23:1—translated "The Lord is my shepherd; I shall not want"—and to my mind, their most astonishing aspect is passed over almost universally. Our eye and our spiritual sensibilities, it seems, are trained to be drawn more to the pastoral image of what God does in shepherding us than to the simple truth of *who* is doing the shepherding. But the identity of the shepherd is no small thing.

He is "the Lord." Of all the beautiful words in the psalm, what David is claiming with these first two words is the most staggering.

It is one thing to have a shepherd. That is wonderful. But everyone has shepherds. "The fact is that we are all followers, swept along by a flow of circumstances and experiences and ideas and people. Even our best attempts to swim against the tide are strangely conformist."[1] We are each following someone or something all the time; we're relying on someone or something other than ourselves to keep us safe and protect us and to provide the comfort we need to face life unafraid.

To be told here, however, that it is "the LORD" who shepherds us should stop us in our tracks. As W. Phillip Keller says, "Our view of Him is often too small—too cramped—too provincial—too human."[2] In moving so quickly past the significance of the shepherd's name in verse 1, we lose the deepest beauty of the verse in two ways: we dull the splendor of what it means for this one to be, incredibly, *a* shepherd; and we miss the loveliness of what it means for him to be *my* shepherd.

You will notice that "LORD" is in large and small capital letters. King David here calls God by his personal name. In Hebrew it consists of four letters transliterated as *YHWH*, and in English it is often written as *Yahweh*. This is God's covenant name, the name God gave to Moses straight after the dramatic encounter with him at the burning bush in Exodus 3. What Moses saw there was part of the visual illustration of what it means for God to be God (the other part of the illustration being the events of the exodus themselves, which would also fill out the content of the divine name). Moses asked God what he should say to the people of Israel if they asked him for the name of the God who

---

1   Mike Cain, *Real Life Jesus: Meaning, Freedom, Purpose* (Nottingham, UK: Inter-Varsity Press, 2008), 142.

2   W. Phillip Keller, *A Shepherd Looks at Psalm 23* (Grand Rapids, MI: Zondervan, 1970), 2. Another nice exception to the surprising neglect of this detail is David B. Calhoun, *A Sheep Remembers* (Edinburgh: Banner of Truth, 2021), 8–11.

had sent Moses to them (v. 13). "God said to Moses, 'I am who I am.' And he said, 'Say this to the people of Israel: 'I am has sent me to you'" (v. 14).

This unusual self-presentation of God, both in picture (a burning bush that was not consumed) and in words ("I am who I am"), means several important things for us. It means that, as many commentators point out, God is profoundly mysterious. "By giving us his name, God lets us know who he is. But God's name is so hard to comprehend—so inscrutable—that it forces us to admit that there are some things about God that we will never understand."[3] So, already we need to add something to the easily understandable and very relatable image of God as a shepherd: the one who is my shepherd is one whom I cannot, in fact, ever fully understand.

This takes on even greater significance when we consider the words of Exodus 3 in relation to the picture of Exodus 3. While scholars debate the best possible translation of "I am who I am"—whether it could or should be translated as "I am who I will be" or "I will be who I will be"—what is clear is that this unusual rendering of the Hebrew verb meaning "to be" points to "One who remains constant because he is independent."[4] Here is God telling Moses that to be God is to be completely and utterly other than us. He is who he is without us. He is eternally who he is from before we were until after we have been. And he is who he is despite our life circumstances.

---

3 Philip G. Ryken, *Exodus: Saved for God's Glory*, Preach the Word (Wheaton, IL: Crossway, 2015), 86.

4 Joel R. Beeke and Paul M. Smalley, *Reformed Systematic Theology*, vol. 1, *Revelation and God* (Wheaton, IL: Crossway, 2019), 554.

When I came to be me, I owed the origin of my life to my parents and the maintenance of my life to the resources of the natural world around me. I have never been able to say that I just "am," or even that I just "will be," because the very essence of being human is to be a dependent creature. But God is revealing to Moses that his name "the LORD" means that none of those things about me are true of him. God is who he is simply by virtue of being himself. His existence is *from* himself and *for* himself, and there is nothing about him that is derived in any way from anyone else. God is absolutely self-sufficient self-existence, and he is your shepherd.

Perhaps we need the picture of the burning bush to seal the significance of it all. It is true, of course, that fire symbolizes the holiness of God, and this is undeniably a major aspect of what Moses encounters as he witnesses the flames: "Do not come near; take your sandals off your feet, for the place on which you are standing is holy ground" (Ex. 3:5). I believe this facet of what it means to name "the LORD" as our shepherd is also really important in Psalm 23, as we will see when we come to verse 3.

However, the main point of the bush burning with fire yet not being consumed by fire is precisely to illustrate what we have seen above about God's self-existent nature. As Sinclair Ferguson says: "The fire that was in the bush was not dependent on the bush for its energy to burn. It was a most pure fire, a fire that was nothing but fire, a fire that was not a compound of other energy sources but had its energy source in itself."[5] Moses was given a vivid visual aid to teach him that the Lord is the God who "has all life, glory, goodness, blessedness, in and of himself; and is alone in and unto

---

5 Sinclair Ferguson, sermon excerpt in Timothy Brindle, "Self-Sufficiency," (bonus) track 14 on Shai Linne, *The Attributes of God*, Lamp Mode Recordings, 2011.

himself all-sufficient, not standing in need of any creatures which he has made."[6]

I tell the Trinity Church family often that the best thing I can ever give them from the pulpit is a clearer sight of God himself and that the greatest thing they can ever have in life is more of God himself. We always want practical religion—effective habits, daily disciplines, lifestyle fixes—and these can all be wonderful if they are full of gospel grace, but the fountain from which they flow is God himself. Whoever you are, and whatever you are experiencing today as you read these lines, there is nothing better to know in all the world than that the shepherd you belong to is the Lord of the burning bush who revealed his name to Moses.

This point is so rich it is worth taking time to linger over it. Consider these words of Alexander Maclaren:

> The fire that burns and does not burn out, which has no tendency to destruction in its very energy, and is not consumed by its own activity, is surely a symbol of the One Being, whose being derives its law and its source from itself, who can only say—"I am that I am"—the law of his nature, the foundation of his being, the only conditions of his existence being, as it were, enclosed within the limits of his own nature. You and I have to say, "I am that which I have become," or "I am that which I was born," or "I am that which circumstances have made me." He said, "I am that I am." All other creatures are links; this is the staple from which they all hang. All other being is derived, and therefore limited and changeful; this being is underived,

---

6   Westminster Confession of Faith 2.2.

absolute, self-dependent, and therefore unalterable forevermore. Because we live, we die. In living, the process is going on of which death is the end. But God lives forevermore. A flame that does not burn out; therefore his resources are inexhaustible, his power unwearied. He needs no rest for recuperation of wasted energy. His gifts diminish not the store which he has to bestow. He gives and is none the poorer. He works and is never weary. He operates unspent; he loves and he loves forever. And through the ages, the fire burns on, unconsumed and undecayed.[7]

Here is the point of this meandering start to our study of Psalm 23: the one whom you need to shepherd you neither needs you nor needs to be shepherded himself as he gives himself to shepherd you. He shepherds you from his eternally undiminishing fullness, and he is never the poorer for it.

Look how needy David is in Psalm 23. If the Lord is his shepherd, then he is of course portraying himself as sheep-like in all the things he needs. He requires food, rest, water, guidance, shelter, comfort, housing, helping. You name it, David needs it. And here is the question Psalm 23 asks: Can you see who gives David all that he needs? It is the God who needs nothing and no one. The one who essentially says to his people: "'I AM WHO I AM.' Before you were, I was, and after you are no more, I will be. I am the first, I am the last, I am a God outside time before time began." So in this psalm, David comes alongside you as you read and puts his strong shepherd crook around your shoulder and pulls you in so that you can hear him tell you that the God of heaven can

---

7 Alexander Maclaren, *Expositions of Holy Scripture*, 11 vols. (Grand Rapids, MI: Eerdmans, 1952–1959), 1:23–24; cited in Ryken, *Exodus*, 87–88.

meet your every need precisely because he is the one who has no need of anything himself.

This is where the next phrase in verse 1 (which we will come to in a moment) receives all its meaning: "I shall not want." Despite my best intentions and my most fervent wishes, I am not the kind of father whose children are able to say, every day, for the rest of their lives, "I shall not want." I might love them very much and pray for them always and long for their best, but I am a finite, sinful man with limited resources on every hand. I cannot supply their every need as I shepherd them through life. But God is not like that with us. It is one thing to have a shepherd, but it is an utterly staggering thing to have as a shepherd the one who is strength itself, who never tires, never slumbers, and who never needs protection himself. In the words of John Mason's wonderful hymn:

> How great a being, Lord, is thine,
> which doth all beings keep!
> Thy knowledge is the only line
> to sound so vast a deep.
> Thou art a sea without a shore,
> a sun without a sphere;
> thy time is now and evermore,
> thy place is everywhere.[8]

So here is where we touch the wonder of the fact that this one, a God like this, the Lord, might ever be described as a shepherd. Just consider for a moment: What kind of pictures does the idea of

8   John Mason, "How Shall I Sing That Majesty?" (1683), https://hymnary.org/.

complete and utter self-sufficient, self-existent deity conjure up in your mind? I think you would agree that this aspect of who God is lends itself most naturally to pictures of strength and power. Indeed, as Kenneth Bailey shows in his wonderful book *The Good Shepherd*, the images used for God throughout the Psalter have a distinctive "homeland security" ring to them. The dominant metaphors are *shield, high tower, fortress, high place, refuge, rock, stronghold, horn of salvation.*[9]

Yet, at the same time, Bailey notes how the Psalter also uses three other metaphors for God—*shepherd* (Ps. 23); *mother* (Ps. 131); *father* (Ps. 103)—and he argues persuasively that when the Lord Jesus wants powerfully to depict who God is toward his weak and wayward people, it is "no accident that the trilogy of parables in Luke 15:1–31 centers on a *good shepherd*, a *good woman* and a *good father*."[10] In John's Gospel, the Lord Jesus declares, "I am the good shepherd" (John 10:11). It is a familiar title we know and love, and we are right to see him as the true fulfillment of what it means to call the Lord our shepherd. But in doing so we must remember what Jesus also declared a few chapters earlier in John: "Jesus said to them, 'Truly, truly, I say to you, before Abraham was, I am'" (John 8:58). This is an astonishing claim. Jesus took the divine name that God revealed to Moses in the burning bush and he effectively applied it to himself: "I am the LORD." The Lord Jesus, our good shepherd, is Yahweh himself, which means he is our sufficient shepherd.

---

9   Kenneth E. Bailey, *The Good Shepherd: A Thousand-Year Journey from Psalm 23 to the New Testament* (London: SPCK, 2015), 35. See Ps. 18, for instance, where most of these images are used together for cumulative effect.

10 Bailey, *The Good Shepherd*, 37 (emphasis original).

I hope you can see new layers of beauty to the simple phrase "The LORD is my shepherd." It is a portrait to communicate that the one at your side has matchless strength and indescribable power, which he is stooping to lend to your aid. As Bailey says, this psalm expresses a profound commitment to God "as the source of security in the midst of many dangers where no other help is available."[11] The self-sufficient God is not the self-absorbed God. The self-existent God is not the self-centered God. Rather—wonder of wonders—the God who is so strong clothes himself in a picture of the closest tender care for those who are so weak. It is a way of saying that he puts all the resources of his infinite fullness at the disposal of finite creatures. He is a shepherd. As Martin Luther says:

> The other names sound somewhat too gloriously and majesti-cally, and bring, as it were, an awe and fear with them, when we hear them uttered. This is the case when Scripture calls God our Lord, King, Creator. This, however, is not the case with the sweet word *shepherd*. It brings to the godly, when they read it or hear it, as it were, a confidence, a consolation, or security like the word *father*.[12]

More than this, he is *my* shepherd. In fact, this too is part of the meaning of the divine name revealed to Moses. Theologians

---

11 Bailey, *The Good Shepherd*, 38. He suggests that, in the many dangers on the open pasturelands of the Middle East, saying "The Lord is my shepherd" means, among other things, "I have no police protection" (37).

12 Cited in William S. Plumer, *Psalms: A Critical and Expository Commentary with Doctrinal and Practical Remarks* (Edinburgh: Banner of Truth, 1975), 309.

are right to say that this divine name "reveals God's *covenant lordship*."[13]

Immediately before the words in Exodus 3:14, where God says he is "I AM WHO I AM," Moses asks God, "Who am I that I should go to Pharaoh and bring the children of Israel out of Egypt?" (Ex. 3:11). God's answer is not to reveal something persuasive about Moses to bolster his confidence; rather, he reveals something about himself: "But I will be with you, and this shall be the sign for you, that I have sent you: when you have brought the people out of Egypt, you shall serve God on this mountain" (Ex. 3:12). God's name means that he is the sovereign Lord and that he is faithful to his covenant relationships. Who God is coordinates with what God does. "God also said to Moses, 'Say this to the people of Israel, "The LORD, the God of your fathers, the God of Abraham, the God of Isaac, and the God of Jacob has sent me to you"'" (Ex. 3:15). Moses is learning that God has his whole family tree in his hand. God is telling Moses that he is the God who goes way back beyond Moses, way back to his fathers, and indeed he is the God who existed way back even before them. The point is that "God's sovereign independence supports and enables his faithfulness to keep his covenant. Therefore, we can depend upon God to be faithfully present with his people throughout history."[14] Moses learns that the sovereign Lord is also the covenant Lord. As one Puritan summarized it, "What I was to them, the same will I be to you."[15]

---

13 Beeke and Smalley, *Reformed Systematic Theology*, 1:551 (emphasis original).
14 Beeke and Smalley, *Reformed Systematic Theology*, 1:558.
15 John Preston, *Life Eternall, or, A Treatise on the Divine Essence and Attributes*, 2nd ed. (London, 1631), pt. 1, 96, cited in Beeke and Smalley, *Reformed Systematic Theology*, 1:558.

Our relationship with God through the Lord Jesus has the deepest possible foundations. We take our place today in world history downstream of God's covenant promises to his people to be with them and to be their God. So our relationship with God is never purely individual and personal, even though it is also never less than that. It is always so much more. The fact that Jesus is a shepherd is wonderful, but the fact that he can be my shepherd is based on his drawing me in personally to a covenant relationship that predated me and will outlast me. The scale of that covenant relationship means I can know he is mine because it is the very meaning of his name to be the God who is faithful to his people.

This profoundly personal aspect to Psalm 23 is very precious. One of the hardest and saddest things I do is take funerals of people who know nothing about the shepherd yet who want the Shepherd's Psalm at their funeral. They have in mind verse 4:

Even though I walk through the valley of the shadow of
    death,
    I will fear no evil,
for you are with me;
    your rod and your staff,
    they comfort me.

Psalm 23 has become a funeral psalm. But, in fact, it is really a psalm about life. Only one verse out of six speaks about death. The imagery of the psalm is dominated with food, water, rest, security; it's about going to a banquet where you have perfumed oil poured on your head and you have a cup of wine in your hand, where you have to say to the host, "No, stop, it's overflowing!"

Psalm 23 is about abundant life. It is more about the happiness of living than the sadness of dying, and all of the happiness is bound up with being able to say that this Lord who is a shepherd is also *my* shepherd.

There is a famous story about a young shepherd boy in the Scottish Highlands in centuries past. His parents died prematurely, leaving the boy in the care of his grandfather, a shepherd. The grandson was raised to be a shepherd too, but he was uneducated. He never went to school and he was unable to read. His grandfather taught him the first five words of Psalm 23 by taking the boy's left hand and, as he said each word, pointing to a finger. Soon the boy could say the words himself, holding one finger and then the next as he did so: "The—LORD—is—my—shepherd."

On one occasion when the boy was out in the hills tending the sheep, a terrible blizzard swept in, engulfing the mountains, and the boy and the sheep did not return home. His grandfather set out to find him, but the brutal winds and blinding snow made that impossible. He knew he would soon lose all sense of direction and so, fearful and heartsore, he returned to spend a long and restless night in his chair. When at last he was able to search the hills, tragically, he found his grandson frozen to death in the snow. But as he stooped to lift the child, he noticed that the boy's hands were clasped in a peculiar way. His right hand firmly gripped the fourth finger of his left hand: "The LORD is *my* shepherd."[16]

My calling as a pastor is always to ask people where they are with this shepherd. The members of my congregation are asked all the time by others about their status in relation to something

16 A full version of this story is available at https://www.fahanchurch.org/the23rdpsalm .htm, accessed March 2, 2022.

or someone: their vaccine status? their relationship status? their employment status? But the pastor's job is to ask about flock status: Are you a sheep who knows the shepherd?

If you can say that he is *your* shepherd, then I want to show you in what follows that you have everything you will ever need.

2

What He Provides

IN OUR TRINITY CHURCH FAMILY, on the first Sunday of every year, we say questions and answers 1 and 2 of the Heidelberg Catechism:

Lord's Day 1

1. *What is your only comfort in life and death?*
    That I am not my own, but belong—body and soul, in life and in death—to my faithful Saviour Jesus Christ. He has fully paid for all my sins with his precious blood, and has set me free from the tyranny of the devil. He also watches over me in such a way that not a hair can fall from my head without the will of my Father in heaven: in fact, all things must work together for my salvation. Because I belong to him, Christ, by his Holy Spirit, assures me of eternal life and makes me wholeheartedly willing and ready from now on to live for him.

2. *What must you know to live and die in the joy of this comfort?*
Three things: first, how great my sin and misery are; second, how I am set free from all my sins and misery; third, how I am to thank God for such deliverance.

Like Psalm 23, these elevated words have comforted God's people for generations. But they are not merely striking words; they are also a profound confession of faith. They are words that express our trust in God and the beautiful implications of what it means to know him. Observe how the catechism begins with a declaration of trust in God's total care: body and soul, in life and in death, physical and spiritual. Every part of life is in God's wise and good hands.

Psalm 23 is a Hebrew version of the Heidelberg Catechism long before the catechism was ever written. If being able to say that the Lord is his shepherd is David's personal testimony, then he expresses the meaning of that relationship with three great confessions of faith, three confidently expressed implications of knowing the Lord: "I shall not want"—for you are my shepherd (v. 1); "I will fear no evil"—for you are my companion (v. 4); and "I shall dwell in the house of the LORD forever"—for you are my host (v. 6). The psalm is an expression of total trust in God's total care.

It is quite something to be able to say, as David says, "I shall not want."

Really? You shall not want? Honestly?

I want all the time. I'm sure you do too. Want is all around us; in our hearts, we all want things. Better health. Better bodies. New bodies. We want good grades, better jobs, better salaries, better

better relationships. I want peace and quiet. A vacation. An end of the pandemic. An end of war. So how are we to understand David's confident assertion here? We need to do so in a way that is realistic and honest and that does not leave us singing tired clichés and empty platitudes about God being all we want when we obviously want so many other things too. There are many layers to this which will help us understand these words.

The first step is to note that, although made up of only four words in Hebrew, verse 1 contains an implicit logical flow: "The LORD is my shepherd; *therefore* I shall not want." *Because* the Lord is my shepherd, I lack for nothing. If I have him, I have everything. He is mine; so I have all I need. This is a profoundly God-centered view of life, the universe, and everything in it. If Psalm 23 says so much in only six verses, then even more amazing is the fact that, in a sense, verses 2–6 are merely an expansion on verse 1. The whole psalm is there in one verse. Each of the other verses simply fills out what it means to belong to a God like this.

As part of this attentiveness to the words and flow of verse 1, we should also recognize the potential here for our English translations to lead us somewhat astray. Although not listed as a translation issue in the ESV footnotes for this psalm, the word for "want" would be better rendered as "lack." The word "want" in the translation has come down to us from the King James Version of the Bible, where the Elizabethan word meant not so much to desire something as to lack it, as in the phrase "to be found wanting." Harold Kushner, a Jewish Rabbi, argues for a translation like this: "I shall lack for nothing." The meaning, he explains, is that "God will provide me with everything I need. Or as a colleague of mine beautifully rendered it, 'The Lord is my shepherd, what more do I need?' The issue of whether I desire things beyond that is beside the point."[1]

The sense, then, as Richard Briggs puts it so well, is that "verse 1 points to letting YHWH decide what it is I need, in the very process of ensuring that whatever it is, I will not lack it. . . . Psalm 23 is partly in the business of training my sense of need to be better attuned to what God provides."[2] This psalm is a tool in God's hand—we might say the tool is a staff—which he uses to recalibrate our desires. Kenneth Bailey suggests that our very conception of wants suffers from our presence in capitalistic societies where "the entire economic system is built on creating and then satisfying as many perceived wants as possible. . . . The goal appears to be: Create *wants* and then turn them into *felt needs*."[3] Psalm 23, however, is an oasis in our materialistic wasteland. It invites us to stop and rest awhile, and consider afresh who God is for us in the simple plenitude of his being and the endless riches of his covenant love. David, it seems, knew in advance what the apostle Paul would later describe as the ability to live "having nothing, and yet possessing everything" (2 Cor. 6:10).

With this in mind, I think the next layer is simply to luxuriate in the picture given to us in Psalm 23:2–3. Before we try to

---

1   Harold S. Kushner, *The Lord Is My Shepherd: Healing Wisdom of the Twenty-Third Psalm* (New York: Knopf, 2003), 29. Kushner tells of a sign he once saw in a shop window: "If we don't have it, you're better off without it." He adds: "The message of the psalm would seem to be that, if you don't have something, no matter how much you crave it, you don't really need it. If you needed it, God would have provided you with it" (30).

2   Richard S. Briggs, *The Lord Is My Shepherd: Psalm 23 for the Life of the Church* (Grand Rapids, MI: Baker Academic, 2021), 73–74.

3   Kenneth E. Bailey, *The Good Shepherd: A Thousand-Year Journey from Psalm 23 to the New Testament* (London: SPCK, 2015), 38–39 (emphasis original).

analyze it, we should feel it. Regardless of their Middle Eastern origins related to animal husbandry, the words in these verses have continued to speak a universal language of beautiful rest and whole-person restoration. Take in the images. The shepherd provides food (green pastures) and drink (still waters), and the fact that he makes me lie down there means there is more than enough in that place. The sheep doesn't need to go drifting off to other places for more food; that can all be obtained from the place where the shepherd has led me. This place of bounteous feeding and secure resting means that "he restores my soul" (v. 3).

Perhaps it is true, as many commentators tell us, that it is very hard indeed to make a sheep lie down. They are normally seen up on their feet, busy and active and wandering creatures; but there is a kind of rest that comes from knowing that the shepherd is near and so you may safely lie down. You are in the presence of someone who is just taking care of everything. Notice how in verses 2–3, there are four verbs of which the Lord is the subject, the one doing all the work: *he makes* me, *he leads* me, *he restores*, *he leads* me.

I was once a guest in a luxurious five-star hotel. Anytime I enquired at the front desk for something, I was asked, "May I have the pleasure of your name, Sir?" The people doing the caring wanted to relate to me personally so they could best provide what I needed. My every need was taken care of in its entirety, no matter how big or how small. Nothing I ever wanted was too much trouble, and they were doing it for me individually and personally.

The power of these shepherding images combining to portray beautiful rest should be enjoyed. Kushner asks why we are so drawn to mountains and seashore when we choose a vacation destination, or why we can sit by a lake for an hour or more and leave feeling relaxed? He answers:

> God's world, decorated in blues and greens, calms us, gently bathing our eyes with quiet, low-intensity colors. We spend so much of our lives in a man-made environment, with its artificial lighting and artificial cooling and heating, bright neon signs and color television programs, that when we get a day off . . . we instinctively feel the need to find our way to God's world with its more restful palette.[4]

Kushner goes on to argue that the invention of electricity has led humankind to rule the night as we rule the day, the ability to dispel darkness leading to our sense of mastery over the world, but "in the process it alienated many of us from the natural world. We spend more of our waking hours under bright lights than we do in God's world of blue skies and green grass."[5] I suggest this is why, in part, we find the language of Psalm 23 so captivating. It expresses in so few words not just the capacity we have for rest but also the vast longing of the human heart for true, profound and long-lasting rest in a wearisome world.

All of this, however, raises the question of practical application. What does it actually mean to have this kind of sensory experience from the hand of the good shepherd? Apart from anything else, the logic of the opening verses is that because the Lord is mine, I lack for nothing *and* I have his provision—physically, spiritually, emotionally—so that I am completely at rest. So the images of green

4 Kushner, *The Lord Is My Shepherd*, 39.
5 Kushner, *The Lord Is My Shepherd*, 41.

grass, still waters, and restored soul speak to a sense of whole-person refreshment that the Lord Jesus, our good shepherd, brings. They are word pictures for the totality of his care. In short, they are what it *feels* like to be shepherded by him. But what does this actually look like in everyday life? Richard Briggs is right to say that "the Psalm does *not* end with 'I will dwell in a lovely café at the end of the day.' It is not sponsored by a local walking group."[6]

Here we need to take a step back and widen the lens. A bit of time seeing the big picture will help us receive the deepest and greatest applications from this psalm. Many commentators, both Jewish and Christian, have noted how the metaphor of sheep and shepherd is not a picture plucked out of thin air in the mind of David the poet, nor even one drawn just from his experience as a shepherd. Indeed, Abel, Abraham, Jacob, Joseph, and Moses were shepherds before him and knew God himself to be their shepherd. Consider Psalm 77:19–20, which trumpets God's redemption of his people from Egypt:

> Your way was through the sea,
>> your path through the great waters;
>> yet your footprints were unseen.
> You led your people like a flock
>> by the hand of Moses and Aaron.

At this point we need to observe that in Psalm 23 we are, in fact, hearing beautiful echoes of the exodus story. The metaphor of shepherd and sheep in Psalm 23 is what Peter Craigie calls "a

6 Briggs, *The Lord Is My Shepherd*, 149 (emphasis original).

loaded metaphor" because "the metaphor associates it with the Exodus from Egypt and the Hebrews' travels in the wilderness, when God's provision and protection had been known like that of a Shepherd."[7]

This was not obvious to me in my first reading of Psalm 23, and it may not seem at all obvious to you. But consider the following:

1. When David says in verse 1 that he will not want, or that he will lack for nothing, he uses the same phrase found in Deuteronomy 2:7: "These forty years the LORD your God has been with you. You have lacked nothing." The idea of God's faithful provision is so freighted in Israelite thought with the wilderness experience after the exodus, and God's supplying his people with food and drink in their desert existence, that the use of the same word here is surely meant to recall God's earlier shepherding of his people. This is an example of what Craigie calls "the undertones of the Exodus" in Psalm 23.[8]

2. In Exodus 15:13 we read,

> You have led in your steadfast love the people whom you
>   have redeemed;
>   you have guided them by your strength to your holy
>   abode.

Here the word for "abode" is pasture, the same word as the pastures or meadows in which the Lord makes David lie down. The verb "guide" is used in both passages. The exodus had as

---

7   Peter C. Craigie, *Psalms 1–50*, Word Biblical Commentary (Grand Rapids, MI: Zondervan, 2004), 206.

8   Craigie, *Psalms 1–50*, 206.

its ultimate goal the Lord's safe leading of this people to the promised land, which would be a land flowing with milk and honey, meeting their every need, and where they would dwell secure. David uses the words of that story to describe what his shepherd provides for him.

3. In Psalm 23:2, as the ESV notes, the Hebrew translated "still waters" literally means "beside waters of rest." This idea of arriving at a "resting place" was the goal when the ark of the covenant set out from Sinai in Numbers 10:33. In fact, as James Hamilton observes, the same word is used in Genesis 2:15, which could be rendered "Yahweh took the man and caused him to rest in the garden of Eden."[9] The phrase "resting places" also appears in Deuteronomy 12:9 as a depiction of the promised land, the land of inheritance that God was giving to his people. As Hamilton says: "When David refers to 'waters of resting places' with this term, then, he evokes the way that Yahweh shepherded his people to the good land he promised them. That good land God promised his people was an attempt to renew what was lost when Adam was driven from Eden."[10]

4. We should note that the phrase in Psalm 23:3 "for his name's sake" also associates the psalm with the exodus because it is clear from other parts of Scripture that acting for his own name's sake was the ultimate goal of the Lord's leading and guiding his people out of Egypt.

Yet he saved them for his name's sake,
    that he might make known his mighty power. (Ps. 106:8)

---

9   James M. Hamilton Jr., *Psalms*, vol. 1, Evangelical Biblical Theology Commentary (Bellingham, WA: Lexham, 2021), 295–96.

10   Hamilton, *Psalms*, 296.

The same idea is present in Isaiah 63:12:

> . . . who caused his glorious arm
>   to go at the right hand of Moses,
> who divided the waters before them
>   to make for himself an everlasting name.

I hope these points show that there is, perhaps, more going on in Psalm 23 than we first anticipated. Scripture is, in fact, explicit about the kind of connection I am encouraging us to see:

> He struck down every firstborn in Egypt,
>   the firstfruits of their strength in the tents of Ham.
> Then he led out his people like sheep
>   and guided them in the wilderness like a flock.
> He led them in safety, so that they were not afraid,
>   but the sea overwhelmed their enemies. (Ps. 78:51–53)

Hidden in plain sight, David is casting his own experience of life with the shepherd of Israel in language borrowed from the earlier experience of the Israelite people to say that what God has done for them he is now doing for David too—and it is precisely here that I believe the greatest riches and the clearest, most beautiful sight of the Lord Jesus is to be found.

In their wonderful book *Echoes of Exodus*, Alastair Roberts and Andrew Wilson suggest that "David sang exodus-shaped songs because, from start to finish, he lived an exodus-shaped life."[11] After

---

11 Alastair J. Roberts and Andrew Wilson, *Echoes of Exodus: Tracing Themes of Redemption through Scripture* (Wheaton, IL: Crossway, 2018), 94.

initial triumphs against the representative enemy of God's people—David against Goliath, like Moses against Pharaoh—David, like Moses, ends up wandering in the wilderness, eating the bread of the Presence (like Israel receiving manna from heaven); those he leads grumble against him; and he spends time in a foreign nation living under a foreign king.[12] This means that Psalm 23 is David's own song about what it feels like to be saved by the Lord from his enemies in a hostile world and kept and cared for by the Lord in the midst of his experience of life in a wilderness world, just as God had cared for David's Israelite ancestors. It means that for you and me this is a description of what it feels like to belong to the Lord Jesus as we too journey through this wilderness world, in exodus-shaped lives, on our way to the promised land of the new creation, where we will dwell with God forever.

In Mark's Gospel, immediately after learning of the death of John the Baptist, Jesus says to his apostles, "Come away by yourselves to a desolate place and rest a while" (6:31). Notice immediately the themes of wilderness and rest. But in this desolate place Jesus is greeted by a great crowd. We are told, "He had compassion on them, because they were like sheep without a shepherd" (6:34). Here so many different strands of the overarching biblical story of redemption come together in one place that it is not too strong to say that the Lord Jesus physically enacts the meaning of Psalm 23 for us. It is surely no accident that on seeing the sheep without a shepherd, Jesus commands everyone to "*sit down* in groups on the *green* grass" (Mark 6:39). Jesus then feeds the multitude so completely that

12 Roberts and Wilson, *Echoes of Exodus*, 94–95.

there are twelve basketfuls left over, such is the abundant over-flow of his supply.

Yet, by doing all this immediately after the death of John at the hands of Herod (who is a bad shepherd of Israel, a false shepherd, and who has just hosted a banquet of death), Jesus feeds his sheep "in the presence of [his] enemies" knowing what fate will befall him and his followers. His disciples, however, resemble Israel in the wilderness, as Psalm 78 portrays them:

> They tested God in their heart
>   by demanding the food they craved.
> They spoke against God, saying,
>   "Can God spread a table in the wilderness?
> He struck the rock so that water gushed out
>   and streams overflowed.
> Can he also give bread
>   and provide meat for his people?" (vv. 18–20)[13]

By proving to his hard-hearted disciples again and again that he is able to provide for their every need, Jesus is enacting in Mark's Gospel what he explicitly states in John's Gospel: "I am the door. If anyone enters by me, he will be saved and he will go in and out and find pasture" (John 10:9). The green pastures of rest that Psalm 23 depicts are the pastures of rest that humanity has been longing for ever since our exile from Eden; they are a restoration to us of what has been lost through our sin and rebellion, and

---

13 I am indebted here to the excellent work of Kenneth Bailey, *The Good Shepherd*, 153–86. Bailey gives a compelling presentation of how the flow of Ps. 23 is mirrored almost exactly in the flow of Mark 6:7–52 (see esp. 175).

they return to us only as we place ourselves within the care of Jesus our shepherd.

James Hamilton says, "Those whom Yahweh shepherds will be led to the place where all God's promises are realized, all needs met, and all fears gone."[14] Although we are still journeying to the new heavens and the new earth, all God's promises are realized in the Lord Jesus. He is the Lord of Psalm 23, the one who is the subject of verb after verb, the one who takes all the initiative for the total care of his flock, the one who provides completely for all our needs, and the one who is able to protect us from all our fears. The exodus-shaped life of God's people throughout the Old Testament becomes, of course, the exodus-shaped life of the Lord Jesus himself, tested in the wilderness for forty days and nights but remaining faithful where all others before him had failed the test. As the faithful, true Son of God, as the second Adam, as the greater Moses, as great David's greater son, he carries out the true exodus in his life-giving death, with the judgment and wrath of God falling on him as the Passover Lamb instead of his sinful people, and in so doing he leads us out of our slavery to sin to new life in him.

There are very great depths here in which to anchor your faith. Given the underlying exodus themes in Psalm 23:1–3, Peter Craigie says, "The psalmist is expressing confidence and trust in such a manner that his sentiments are linked to the great acts of divine salvation of the past, which in turn formed the basis of the covenant faith."[15] This is precisely the answer to the kind of question we might ask as we read Psalm 23:1–3 and wonder: *Yes, but what about me? The Lord is my Shepherd, agreed,*

14 Hamilton, *Psalms*, 296.
15 Craigie, *Psalms 1–50*, 206.

but how do I actually experience the same kind of provision David is speaking about here? What does that look like?

The first part of the answer is that we receive deeper help here by thinking about *us* before thinking about *me*. As Roberts and Wilson say: "Much of the contemporary church, especially in evangelical circles, suffers from a rootlessness that makes it easy to lose our bearings, and even our identity. We live in a disoriented and rootless age."[16] But my own relationship with the Lord Jesus is part of an exodus-story relationship that is shared with all other believers. David sings exodus songs not just because of his own exodus-shaped life but also because they are the songs of his people, his ancestors. And we sing exodus songs for the same reason. The song of victory in Exodus 15, for instance, is not just a song that God's people of old sang; it is *our* song too because the people God redeemed are our ancestors in the faith. David's exodus song in Psalm 23 is our song because he is our ancestor in the faith.

Every time we sing Psalm 23, we are celebrating the rescue that God has provided for us in the Lord Jesus through his sinless life and his death on the cross, along with the rest that he offers us through the gospel in this life and the life to come. Every time we read or sing Psalm 23, we are inside the glorious truth that what God has always done for his covenant people he will do for you and me. David's expectation that the Lord will provide for him in all these ways "is based upon something more solid than his own past experience; the undertones of the Exodus indicate that his expectation is established on the bedrock of Israel's faith, namely the precedent of God's refreshment and guidance in the Exodus and wilderness

16 Roberts and Wilson, *Echoes of Exodus*, 14.

journeys."[17] In other words, what God has done already for his people (led them out of Egypt and provided for them in the wilderness) shows me there are more than sufficient grounds to believe that he can do the same for me: God has a track record I can rely on because he's already done it for my family in the faith. I can trust his track record of keeping and leading his people as he leads me from this world to the next with Jesus as my good shepherd.

The green pastures that David is picturing here are found and experienced only as we find ourselves in relationship with Jesus the good shepherd. Jesus said that we find such pastures by "going in and out," with him as the door. This kind of rest comes from an easy familiarity with the presence of the Lord Jesus. We find "green pastures" when in everyday life we are always coming to him and walking with him and being led by him.

This brings us full circle to David's first confession of faith in Psalm 23: "I shall not want" or, better, "I shall lack nothing" (v. 1). As you read these lines, there are likely very many things in life you want. They may be good things to want or bad things to want or unwise things to want; but Psalm 23 teaches you there is nothing you need that Jesus will not supply.

As Matthew Henry puts it, "The greatest abundance is but a dry pasture to a wicked man, who relishes only in that which pleases the senses; but to a godly man, who tastes the goodness of God in all his enjoyments, and by faith relishes that, though he has but little of the world, it is a green pasture."[18]

---

17 Craigie, *Psalms 1–50*, 207.

18 Matthew Henry, *Matthew Henry's Commentary*, vol. 3 (Peabody, MA: Hendrickson, 1991), 258; cited in David B. Calhoun, *A Sheep Remembers* (Edinburgh: Banner of Truth, 2021), 27.

3

Where He Leads

WE HAVE NOW SEEN THAT THERE are exodus echoes in Psalm 23. Twice in verses 1–3 we are told that the shepherd "leads me," and this phrase is a clear exodus undertone in the psalm:

> You have led in your steadfast love the people whom you
>   have redeemed;
>   you have guided them by your strength to your holy
>   abode. (Ex. 15:13)

The point of the journey is the destination—God's dwelling place—and it is no coincidence of course that Psalm 23 ends in the same way:

> and I shall dwell in the house of the LORD
>   forever. (v. 6)

We will come to those beautiful words soon, but for now we want to consider the shape that God's care takes in these opening verses of the psalm. There is both a picture of total, ultimate rest and a picture of the shepherd leading, with us following behind him on his righteous paths. He is leading us home, yes, but the way to his house is a scenic route we need to savor.

Nestled between the perfect provision of verse 2, and the righteous paths of verse 3, is the delightful phrase "He restores my soul." The sentence stands alone and can be read either as summarizing the effect of all the care and attention in verse 2 or as an implication of walking in paths of righteousness. Either way the meaning is clear: the result of receiving the shepherd's close attention and of following in the shepherd's way is the restoration of my soul. What might this actually mean?

Jewish commentators are quick to see in the phrase an indication of all that the Sabbath meant for Israel, and many Christian commentators follow suit. As Richard Briggs says (of vv. 1–3 as a whole): "The logic of these verses is comparable to that of the Sabbath in that both seek to describe a bigger picture of life in all its fullness that helps to gain a wise and proper perspective on the work to be done or the trials to be endured."[1] Again, the connections here to the exodus are considerable when we remember that in Deuteronomy 5 the specific reason the Israelites are given for Sabbath observance was their experience of slavery in a land where they had no rest. Just as God redeemed them from slavery in his mercy and compassion, so they too must ensure that all others within their care are treated with the same mercy and compassion and given the rest of the Sabbath (see Deut. 5:12–15). Alongside this, in Exodus 31, where *creation* is given as the foundational

---

1 Richard S. Briggs, *The Lord Is My Shepherd: Psalm 23 for the Life of the Church* (Grand Rapids, MI: Baker Academic, 2021), 145.

basis for observing the Sabbath, we learn that the day is "a sign forever between me and the people of Israel that in six days the LORD made heaven and earth, and on the seventh day he rested and was refreshed" (v. 17).

If the idea of the Sabbath as an undertone to Psalm 23:1–3 seems far removed from what we personally have ever experienced on that particular day of the week, then again it is worth stepping back and learning more from those who have reflected deeply on the matter. In Abraham Joshua Heschel's classic Jewish text *The Sabbath*, he argues for the idea of an "architecture of holiness" that is present not in space but in time, so that "the Sabbaths are our great cathedrals." The idea is that Sabbath was always intended by God to be a foretaste of paradise, such that when God enters the rest of the seventh day after creating the world, it is the only day of the seven-day week about which we are *not* told, "And there was evening, and there was morning." The Sabbath continues forever in God's presence such that entering this rest with him and enjoying him forever is the goal of all creation. You do not rest on the Sabbath to be refreshed for work; rather, the point of all labor and work is for the sake of the Sabbath: "It is not an interlude but the climax of living."[2]

The provision of the Sabbath as a way of realizing the whole point of creation—rest with God—is profoundly beautiful. It was to be a day of delight for God's people (Isa. 58:13) precisely because it was a time devoted to taking delight in the Lord (Isa. 58:14). The key idea here, which I believe is implied in Psalm 23, is spending time with the Lord, who has already entered into

2   Abraham Joshua Heschel, *The Sabbath: Its Meaning for Modern Man* (New York: Farrar, Straus and Giroux, 1951), 14.

his rest and who therefore invites others to share it with him. As Briggs says, "Psalm 23 also invites us to a slowing of the pace of life and to a rest that might even get as far as stopping completely, laying down, and knowing that life will move on . . . but also rejoicing in the restoration that YHWH the shepherd offers."[3] Heschel expresses it even more poetically: the Sabbath is about coming "to understand that the world has already been created and will survive without the help of man."[4]

This means that Christian readings of Psalm 23 offer many layers to understanding our soul restoration. On the most obvious level of opening Psalm 23 and simply following in David's footsteps, there is a restoration of the soul that takes place when I cease striving to master the world and I am content to lay down the tools of work and instead be nourished by the provision of the shepherd. Sheep benefit enormously from regular, daily, weekly reminders that we are sheep and not the shepherd. A renewal of the soul takes place in seeing afresh who I am in the world—not master and commander but a frail and prone-to-wander sheep with a good shepherd—and that my experience of soul rest will always be dependent on my proximity to him.

The idea of time for soul restoration is so important and is the main way to express the fact that what David is celebrating in verses 1–3 is that he is not the one carrying out the main activity in his life. The shepherd is the primary agent in his life: making him rest, leading him, restoring him, leading him again. Harold Kushner tells the story of tourists on safari in Africa who hired porters to carry their supplies while they trekked. After

3 Briggs, *The Lord Is My Shepherd*, 148.
4 Heschel, *The Sabbath*, 13.

three days the porters told their employers they would need to stop and rest for a day, not because they were tired but because "we have walked too far too fast and now we must wait for our souls to catch up."[5]

Whether we stick to the word "soul" (as Kushner and others do), in the sense of being an interior part of us, or we understand the word "soul" as a stand-in word for the whole person (as I think we are right to do), the fact is that we know what it is like to experience fragmentation within ourselves or within the various components of our lives such that one bit of us has gone "too far too fast" ahead of other parts of who we are, and we are in need of being made whole again. When we move too quickly through life, we tend to make poorer choices, we often prioritize the wrong things, and we can begin to equate our very selves with the status we have achieved or the accumulation of possessions we have amassed. In none of those modes of unreflective living is there space to say, "The LORD is my shepherd; I lack nothing."

Most specifically, it is in coming close to the Lord Jesus that we enter this rest. In Matthew's Gospel, Jesus says: "Come to me, all who labor and are heavy laden, and I will give you rest. Take my yoke upon you, and learn from me, for I am gentle and lowly in heart, and you will find rest for your souls" (Matt. 11:28–29). Jesus is not talking about the kind of rest you get from putting your feet up at the end of a long day. Immediately following these words, he rebuts the Pharisees over the true meaning of the Sabbath (Matt. 12:1–8). No, the point of these

---

5   Harold S. Kushner, *The Lord Is My Shepherd: Healing Wisdom of the Twenty-Third Psalm* (New York: Knopf, 2003), 60.

words is that everything the Sabbath rest pointed to is fulfilled by Jesus himself; the rest that humankind was meant to enter from the very start, and which we still long for, is found in him. The story of the exodus is the story of God's people failing to enter the promised rest. Unlike the unfaithful Israelites who fell in the desert and did not enter their rest (Ps. 95; Heb. 4:1–7), Jesus was faithful unto death and has now entered the Sabbath rest that was the goal of all creation and that we will one day share in with him. "Jesus recapitulated in himself the history of Adam and Israel in order to bring us not only out of ruin into a state of innocence, or guilt into forgiveness, but to bring the whole of creation into the everlasting Sabbath."[6] Our experience of this rest now, in this life, is anticipatory. We enter this Sabbath rest in advance each Lord's Day by believing and treasuring the good news of exodus salvation won for us by the Lord Jesus. In him, and in him alone, we find rest for our souls.

To help us grasp even more what this looks like, Psalm 23:3 tells that the shepherd restores our souls by leading us in his paths of righteousness. This is beautiful for us because, as Alastair Roberts and Andrew Wilson say, "our generation is confused as to the nature of true freedom." We think freedom is found in forging our own path through life and in either "being true to ourselves" or striving to live "the best version of ourselves." But, in fact, "no matter how often we experience liberation from constraints, limitations, and oppression, we still find ourselves falling into new forms of bondage. . . . True freedom is more complicated than

6   Michael Horton, *Lord and Servant: A Covenant Christology* (Louisville: Westminster John Knox, 2005), 220.

it looks."[7] Psalm 23:3 tells us that true freedom is found along someone else's path, not my own.

There are lovely nuances to the phrase rendered "paths of righteousness." Many commentators point out that the "paths" are more literally "cart tracks" or "wagon ruts." The idea is that while "the earth is soft, wagon wheels press the trails that others are obliged to follow after it dries and hardens."[8] When this idea is combined with the strong sense from these verses that the shepherd is leading and is therefore ahead of us, and we are behind him, then whether we understand these tracks as "paths of righteousness" or simply "right paths," as the ESV footnote offers, the point is that they are *his* tracks. The shepherd has gone ahead of us, blazing the trail and leading the way, and therefore the path we are taking is one of righteousness. When we follow the Lord, we cannot fail to be on the right path.

Kenneth Bailey makes the lovely observation that "the good shepherd 'leads me'; he does not 'drive me.'" Because he is ahead and I am following, "the sheep appear to be attracted primarily by the voice of the Shepherd, which they know and are eager to follow."[9] This is of course exactly how the Lord Jesus describes his relationship with his sheep: "When he has brought out all his own, he goes before them, and the sheep follow him, for they know his voice" (John 10:4).

---

7   Alastair J. Roberts and Andrew Wilson, *Echoes of Exodus: Tracing Themes of Redemption through Scripture* (Wheaton, IL: Crossway, 2018), 15.

8   Bruce K. Waltke and James M. Houston, *The Psalms as Christian Worship: A Historical Commentary* (Grand Rapids, MI: Eerdmans, 2010), 439. So too James M. Hamilton Jr., *Psalms*, vol. 1, Evangelical Biblical Theology Commentary (Bellingham, WA: Lexham, 2021), 293–95.

9   Kenneth E. Bailey, *The Good Shepherd: A Thousand-Year Journey from Psalm 23 to the New Testament* (London: SPCK, 2015), 41.

This places the voice of the shepherd right at the heart of what it means to follow the shepherd in his paths of righteousness. Exodus from slavery never meant freedom to do just anything—God redeemed us to be holy. The fire in the burning bush showed the holiness of God's name. The Sabbath given to the people after the exodus was a holy day. Psalm 23 follows the exodus trajectory of grace first, then law; redemption and rescue precede obedience and moral conformity to the beauty of God's law.

This means there is a beautiful connection between righteous paths and wholeness; the way to the restored soul of verse 3 is as much from the right paths as it is from the right food. In other words, happiness is found in holiness. Wholeness is found in righteousness, and this righteousness is found in listening to the voice of the shepherd, attending to his call and heeding his words. In Psalm 19:7, David says,

> The law of the LORD is perfect,
>   reviving the soul.

There is no way to be at rest in this world, or to be at rest with the Lord in the world to come, without being made new by the words he speaks and the righteousness he gives as we give ourselves to him.

So as you read these pages, it is worth taking time to stop and reflect. Take time to rest and consider where you are with the shepherd's paths of righteousness laid out for you in the Scriptures. Our affection for Jesus and our affection for his voice in the Bible are inseparable. We cannot love one without coming to love the other; similarly we cannot neglect our relationship with one and not soon experience a cooling with the other.

Are you on his paths right now but, unbeknownst to anyone else, you are thinking of leaving them? Psalm 23 is clear: there is no soul restoration in walking paths in life that your shepherd is not walking with you. There is no greener grass anywhere else than with Jesus and with the words that he speaks, with his righteous law and his righteousness-giving gospel. But it may be that you have begun to think that the grass really is greener somewhere else even though you know it is a "pasture" where Jesus does not dwell.

It may be that you haven't fully left the paths of righteousness yet but you are flirting with that danger. You are just beginning to wander. Perhaps it's a relationship you know you shouldn't be in: it is not a path of righteousness. Apart from the objective knowledge that it is wrong, one of the ways you are sensing it subjectively is that it has opened up just that little bit of distance between you and the Lord Jesus that wasn't there this time last year. Life is a journey, not a viewing gallery; we are always on the move, always traveling, and we're going with either Jesus's paths or a different shepherd's paths. Maybe it's what you're consuming online. Maybe it's the choices you are making with your money or your time. Two degrees of divergence this year might mean a mile's divergence next year. Take time to consider the road you are walking, who is leading you, and where that path might end. In my experience I have found that wrong steps in life are nearly always the outworking of a prior neglect of listening to Jesus speak in the Bible. When devotion to hearing his voice begins to dwindle, then eventually, inevitably, departure from his paths begins to follow.

Some reading these lines are just beginning to wonder whether following the shepherd is really worth it. For you know full well that the path of the shepherd is the path to the cross. Jesus said, "If anyone would come after me, let him deny himself and take up his cross and follow me" (Mark 8:34). Is it worth all the suffering that following Jesus entails? I want to say that you will not long leave his path before you discover only soul decay and not soul nourishment on any different path. The only way to live is to follow the shepherd into death: "For whoever would save his life will lose it, but whoever loses his life for my sake and for the gospel's will save it" (Mark 8:35). There is a beauty to life with the Lord Jesus that cannot be found anywhere else. What he says in his word is not just true; it is also nourishing and healthy, and only it can make us whole. The cost of following him is the death of all that is ugly and sinful in me—it is painful—but the new life on the other side of my crucified sinful nature is more precious than can be put into words. Life works with Jesus in a way that it just doesn't without him.

The ultimate reason for walking with the shepherd comes at the end of Psalm 23:3. One of the great surprises in the psalm is realizing that the very reason for the vast extent of the shepherd's care for his sheep—both the rest he provides and his righteous paths for them to follow—is the fame of his name, not the fame of his sheep.

It is wonderful to be provided for and to have my every need taken care of by my shepherd, and it is quite something to realize that everything he does for his sheep he does "for his name's sake" (v. 3). He leads by binding his own honor and reputation in his world to his sheep and to what happens to them and how they follow him. As Bruce Waltke and James Houston say, "We live in a universe wherein God's interests and his people's interest cohere, not compete."[10] Or as W. Phillip Keller puts it, "It links a lump of common clay to divine destiny—it means a mere mortal becomes the cherished object of divine diligence."[11]

Again, the depths of this for us are very precious. As we read that the divine shepherd leads us in paths of righteousness for his own name's sake, it means not that God is using us for his own ends but rather that we can be so sure about walking in those paths because God has bound his own reputation to our walking in them. John Piper explains it like this: "The deepest reason given for God's commitment to his people is his prior commitment to his own name. The rock-bottom foundation of our forgiveness and our fearlessness and our joy is the commitment of God to his own great name."[12] We have already seen above the connections of this phrase to the exodus story, where a recurring idea is that God was demonstrating his power to Pharaoh "so that my name may be declared throughout all the earth" (Ex. 9:16), and

he saved them for his name's sake,
    that he might make known his mighty power. (Ps. 106:8)

Remember how at the start of the exodus story neither Moses nor the people of Israel know God's name. Piper comments: "The

---

10 Waltke and Houston, *The Psalms as Christian Worship*, 440.

11 W. Phillip Keller, *A Shepherd Looks at Psalm 23* (Grand Rapids, MI: Zondervan, 1970), 3.

12 John Piper, *The Pleasures of God* (Fearn, Ross-shire, Scotland: Christian Focus, 2001), 100.

point of the Exodus was to make a worldwide reputation for God. The point of the ten plagues and miraculous Red Sea crossing was to demonstrate the astonishing power of God on behalf of his freely chosen people, with the aim that this reputation, this name, would be declared throughout the whole world."[13]

In Psalm 23 I learn that my walking the way of the shepherd—the paths of righteousness, the right path of taking up my cross and following him even unto death—is a journey through life on which God has staked the very honor of his name.

So he will never let me walk alone.

———

The Lord my shepherd rules my life
and gives me all I need;
he leads me by refreshing streams;
in pastures green I feed.

The Lord revives my failing strength,
he makes my joy complete;
and in right paths, for his name's sake,
he guides my faltering feet.

Though in a valley dark as death,
no evil makes me fear;
your shepherd's staff protects my way,
for you are with me there.

13 Piper, *The Pleasures of God*, 101.

While all my enemies look on
you spread a royal feast;
you fill my cup, anoint my head,
and treat me as your guest.

Your goodness and your gracious love
pursue me all my days;
your house, O Lord, shall be my home—
your name my endless praise.

CHRISTOPHER IDLE

PART 2

THE TRAVELER AND
THE COMPANION

Even though I walk through the valley of
the shadow of death,
I will fear no evil,
for you are with me;
your rod and your staff,
they comfort me.

PSALM 23:4

DARKNESS CAN BE FRIGHTENING. But deep darkness, total darkness, can bring unequaled terror to a human soul.

Charles Spurgeon said of Psalm 23:4, "This unspeakably delightful verse has been sung on many a dying bed and has helped to make the dark valley bright."[1] Apart from the opening line of Psalm 23, this verse is undoubtedly the most famous part of the psalm. It is almost certain that these words have already profoundly comforted you at some point in your life. It may be that they are currently the rock beneath your feet in your own approach to death that has drawn unexpectedly nearer, or they have been an anchor for your soul in facing the loss of someone most dear to you. The valleys of the world come in all shapes and sizes, and many of us spend a lot of time in their shadows: bereavement, grief, depression, profound disappointment in life either with ourselves or from the hand of others, pandemic, trauma, and abuse.

In this verse there is a beauty and a balm in almost every word. So I want to help us linger in all its parts so that we can feel the wonder of its assurance.

Although I have called this part of the book "The Traveler and the Companion," it is clear the psalm does not leave the shepherding imagery behind in verse 4. This is evident from the presence of the rod and the staff, implements depicting truly lovely aspects of our good shepherd's work. The flow of the psalm from verses 1–3 into verse 4 makes it obvious that the sheep and the shepherd are still in view here, but it is worth having a focus on the idea of our shepherd as our companion because, in a way, the psalmist wants

1 Charles Spurgeon, *The Treasury of David*, 3 vols. (Peabody, MA: Hendrickson, 1988), 1:355.

to rivet our attention on this facet of the shepherd's care. In the Hebrew of Psalm 23 there are twenty lines (including the title), and line ten—the exact midpoint of the psalm—is this: "for you are with me." So while this verse is sung along a particular road all sheep must take, it is a path they never walk alone.

And the darkness and danger immediately on either side of this centerpiece of complete safety are what make it shine so brightly.

4

How He Leads

UP TO THIS POINT, the sheep in Psalm 23 have been passive. They are being made to lie down and being led and being restored, but now there is the actual movement of the sheep in their walking and going somewhere. And here is where the little phrase that opens the verse ("Even though") signals to us an image ahead that will present the major theological surprise of the verse, and its ultimate comfort. For the journey that one might expect to be making while walking in paths of righteousness (v. 3) is not the movement the psalm actually focuses on in verse 4. Our great familiarity with this psalm as a whole might cause us to miss the stunning way the shepherd leads the sheep for his name's sake.

Take a step back with me for a moment before we zoom in for a close-up look. Consider the fact that we are probably all familiar with Psalm 23 as a recurring feature of the liturgy at funerals. I think I can safely assume that many of the funerals you have attended have included Psalm 23 in some form; but it was not always so.

In a piece entitled "How the Twenty-Third Psalm Became an American Secular Icon," William Holladay has argued that Psalm 23 was not often used in connection with death prior to the American Civil War. Between that time and 1880, however, when it was then regularly used, a series of societal and ecclesial shifts made both highly individualistic and sentimental understandings of religious language more commonplace, so that from the 1900s onward the use of Psalm 23 in funeral services "had become massively widespread."[1] This means that you are as likely to have encountered the psalm at the funeral of an unbeliever as you are at the funeral of someone who knew and loved the Lord Jesus as his or her own shepherd. Holladay identifies several things about Psalm 23 that lend to this:

It is short and therefore easily memorized. It is undemanding. It does not mention sin or suggest the appropriateness of participating in any ecclesial community. It simply seems to affirm that God (or, alternatively, Jesus) accompanies the speaker and takes care of him or her. . . . It is a psalm that could be used in public contexts, acceptable to both Jews and Christians and giving no offense to anyone.[2]

In this way the psalm lends itself to being a "secular icon." It is as if the text is seen as "a badge of good citizenship in the face of death, rather than as a Jewish or Christian affirmation."[3]

---

1   I am relying on Richard S. Briggs's use of Holladay in Briggs, *The Lord Is My Shepherd: Psalm 23 for the Life of the Church* (Grand Rapids, MI: Baker Academic, 2021), 151–52. Cf. William L. Holladay, *The Psalms through Three Thousand Years: Prayerbook of a Cloud of Witnesses* (Minneapolis: Fortress, 1993).

2   Holladay, *Psalms through Three Thousand Years*, 364, cited in Briggs, *The Lord Is My Shepherd*, 152.

3   Briggs, *The Lord Is My Shepherd*, 152.

It is true that God accompanies the speaker and takes care of him or her in a general sense in Psalm 23—and in a culture of religious sentimentality, this is appealing. But come with me for a closer look. In fact, the great surprise is *how* God accompanies the speaker: the sheep is on the move from the Lord's leading on the right paths in verse 3 into his leading in verse 4 onto the valley path. The unexpected development in the story of Psalm 23 is that the good shepherd's paths of righteousness sometimes include the valley of the shadow of death. If I find myself in the valley of deep darkness, it is because he has led me there.

It is clear in this verse that we have not left the shepherd-sheep relationship behind; our companion has a rod and a staff in his hand, and in verse 5 the active verbs will resume to describe the activity of our host toward us as he nourishes us and leads us safely to his dwelling place. It is simply unwise to assume—as some do, unthinkingly—that we have a shepherd who leads us to peace and tranquility but has no say over how sheep come to find themselves in a threatening gorge. No, the valley of the shadow of death, the days of deep darkness, do not mean we have left the paths of righteousness; in fact, they are where the shepherd's paths of righteousness are sometimes located. This is how he leads.

I say this is a surprise because we need to reckon with the terrible intensity of the image that dominates the verse: "the valley of the shadow of death." The commentators tell us that while the translation of the word for "valley" is straightforward, the word translated "shadow of death" is more contested and more complicated. It is a single Hebrew word that can mean "deep darkness" (as the ESV footnote reads). In many other places in the Old

THE TRAVELER AND THE COMPANION

Testament the word is translated as exactly that, for instance in Job 24:17, where it appears twice:

> For deep darkness is morning to all of them;
>> for they are friends with the terrors of deep darkness.[4]

But, as many commentators also realize, it is not as simple as relegating the translation "the valley of the shadow of death" to a bygone but badly judged era of translation whose abiding value lies only in feelings tied to the lyrical power of the King James Version. The fact is, as Peter Craigie observes, that "the expression may have been used deliberately to convey the threat of death," and he points to another text in Job as evidence:

> Are not my days few?
>> Then cease, and leave me alone, that I may find a little cheer
> before I go—and I shall not return—
>> to the land of darkness and deep shadow,
> the land of gloom like thick darkness,
>> like deep shadow without any order,
>> where light is as thick darkness. (Job 10:20–22)[5]

Here the metaphorical idea of deep darkness is very clearly tied to a place of no return: the world of the afterlife. This is death,

4 Briggs, *The Lord Is My Shepherd*, 90.
5 Peter C. Craigie, *Psalms 1–50*, Word Biblical Commentary (Grand Rapids, MI: Zondervan, 2004), 207. Briggs, *The Lord Is My Shepherd*, provides the most detailed recent discussion and, by a different route, also defends the well-known reference to the shadow of death in translation (88–93).

not simply described but poetically depicted, with a choice of (non)color and a concentration that speak immediately to our emotional sense of what dying means. It is a journey away from the light of the known into the obscurity of the unknown, away from the warmth of the sun to the cold of the shade and the shadow. The valley's deep darkness is a perfect metaphor for death's encroachment on life.

Several writers have firsthand experience of valleys of darkness in Palestine, places where "the water often foams and roars, torn by jagged rocks. . . . The path plunges downward . . . into a deep and narrow gorge of sheer precipices overhung by frowning Sphinx-like battlements of rocks, which almost touch overhead. Its side walls rise like the stone walls of a great cathedral."[6] Kenneth Bailey tells of his own encounter with such a place where, in 1957, a flash flood thundered through a deep and narrow gorge, killing some fifty French tourists and giving the literal sense of "the valley of death" to an actual physical place.[7]

We do not know exactly where or what David had in mind as he wrote. But, in a sense, it is the undefined and open-ended nature of the metaphor that is such a help to us. In his day, the terrors of wild animals and bloodthirsty foes were present in the physical valley so that the reality of death crouched at the door for any traveler. In our day, we most likely encounter deep darkness in different ways. Yet, in the same way, death sends its shadow

---

6 Kenneth E. Bailey, *The Good Shepherd: A Thousand-Year Journey from Psalm 23 to the New Testament* (London: SPCK, 2015), 47. Here Bailey is citing the shepherd M. P. Krikorian in his book *The Spirit of the Shepherd: An Interpretation of the Psalm Immortal*, 2nd ed. (Grand Rapids, MI: Zondervan, 1939), 68–69.

7 Bailey, *The Good Shepherd*, 47.

ahead of time across our lives. Richard Briggs builds on the work of Old Testament scholar Jon Levenson to argue that, in ancient poetry, death is understood not in our modern clinical sense of the precise moment the heart stops beating but rather as a malignant terror that casts "its influence (indeed, its 'shadow') even within what we would now call the land of the living."[8] The wise believer knows that from the moment we are born, we are always in the presence of death. It is just that for most of us the shadow has not quite reached us yet; the sun is so high in the sky that we are unaware of it. It can take a valley and the first sight of death's shadow to make us realize that this truth applies to us by name the same as to everyone else. We are always dying.

This idea is also expressed in the unexpected way the punishment of death works out in the book of Genesis. God's prohibition of the tree of the knowledge of good and evil to Adam and Eve contained the warning "for in the day that you eat of it you shall surely die" (2:17). The surprise, of course, is that on the day they ate of it, they did not die. Or did they?

The unfolding story of Scripture reveals that Adam and Eve's death began that day even if it did not arrive in full that day. From the moment they vandalized the garden in their rebellion against their loving heavenly Father, introducing sin into the world, they embarked on a one-way journey to an appointment with death that began to cast its long shadow over the once-perfect creation. As John Calvin says in commenting on Genesis 2:17, "The miseries and evils both of soul and body, with which man is beset so long as he is on earth, are a kind of entrance into death, till

---

8 Briggs, *The Lord Is My Shepherd*, 94.

death itself entirely absorbs him."[9] From the moment of Adam's fall, "death began its reign in him."[10] But the fact that death is so clearly introduced into the world by God himself means that we may say, I think, that the curse of death in the world is God's curse, in the same way that Martin Luther is reported to have said that the devil is God's devil. In other words, God is in charge of them, not they in charge of him. He is not part of the curse, and he is not implicated in the evil works of the devil, yet God is the one ruling the world completely and perfectly.

We will keep thinking about the valley of the shadow of death in the next chapter as we consider the greatest comfort that Psalm 23 offers us. But the point of this chapter is to go slowly enough through the psalm that we absorb the assurance and comfort of knowing it is not possible for the sheep to have an encounter with either death or its advance shadow that is outside God's decree and his loving, fatherly care. My prayer for you as you read these lines is that you come to know the valley you are in to be God's valley and your good shepherd to be the one who has led you there. At this very moment, you might feel more lost than ever, in deepest darkness like a shroud, but your Lord Jesus is not standing there beside you lost or scratching his head wondering what to do. It may not yet be part of your theological framework that all things, including each valley, come from God's fatherly hand. But it needs to be. For if God is not in charge of the valley, how do you know he can get you through it?

9 John Calvin, *Commentaries on the First Book of Moses Called Genesis*, trans. John King, vol. 1 (1847; repr., Grand Rapids, MI: Baker, 1996), 127.

10 Calvin, *Commentaries on the First Book of Moses*, 1:128.

Leland Ryken summarizes the theme of our famous psalm as "the contentment that comes from resting in the sufficiency of God's providence."[11] This is why Christians down the centuries have thought long and hard about how God provides for his people in every single circumstance of life, and the best of such thought has confessed that God leads us to pain as purposefully as he leads us to pleasure. Here are the words of the Heidelberg Catechism once more, this time on the meaning of divine providence:

Lord's Day 10

27. *What do you understand by the providence of God?*
    Providence is the almighty and ever present power of God by which he upholds, as with his hand, heaven and earth and all creatures, and so rules them that leaf and blade, rain and drought, fruitful and lean years, food and drink, health and sickness, prosperity and poverty—all things, in fact, come to us not by chance but from his fatherly hand.

28. *How does the knowledge of God's creation and providence help us?*
    We can be patient when things go against us, thankful when things go well, and for the future we can have good confidence in our faithful God and Father that nothing

---

11 Douglas Sean O'Donnell and Leland Ryken, *The Beauty and Power of Biblical Exposition: Preaching the Literary Artistry and Genres of the Bible* (Wheaton, IL: Crossway, 2022), 176.

will separate us from his love. All creatures are so completely in his hand that without his will they can neither move nor be moved.

Many years ago I remember hearing John Piper advise those teaching in youth ministries that the very best thing they could ever give their young folk was "Big God Theology." The words of the catechism portray just such a big God. It's the God we meet in every part of the Bible's story, from beginning to end. Adam and Eve's fall into sin in the book of Genesis did not take God by surprise or leave him unexpectedly considering his options. He did not send Jesus into the world as Plan B, because he came as the Lamb slain before the foundation of the world (Rev. 13:8). This is the God of Amos 3:6, where the prophet asks,

Does disaster come to a city
  unless the LORD has done it?

God stands behind everything that happens in the world—everything, absolutely everything—but he does not stand behind good and evil in the same way. The disaster that strikes a city is always the Lord's doing, even while he is never the author of evil; he remains in control of everything while he is not tainted in his glory by the evil we do.

Supremely, we see all of this in the valley path our shepherd himself walked throughout his life, a path he traveled to the point of the deepest darkness in his sacrificial death on the cross. In Luke's Gospel, we see the confident claim of the eager follower of Jesus: "I will follow you wherever you go" (9:57). But this assertion comes in a part of the Gospel where it is clear those wanting to follow do not know where Jesus is going. He alone knows he is going to die: "The people did not receive him because his face was set toward Jerusalem" (9:53). The capital city, with its temple mount, will in fact become part of the shepherd's valley descent as he willingly embraces the purpose for which he came: "Now is my soul troubled. And what shall I say? 'Father, save me from this hour'? But for this purpose I have come to this hour" (John 12:27). The shadow of death encompassed his life even before he was born (Matt. 1:21), and at the end he entered the shattering catastrophe of darkness at midday (Matt. 27:45).

But the death of the Lord Jesus displays a stunning truth: his experience of the valley was the work of "lawless men" (Acts 2:23), a despicable deed of delivering him over to death by denying him in the presence of Pilate, who had the power to release him (Acts 3:13), *and at the same time*, this deliverance was "according to the definite plan and foreknowledge of God" (Acts 2:23). The execution of our shepherd as the climax of his lifelong experience of the valley of the shadow of death is the supreme example in Scripture of how God so often leads his children: "You meant evil against me, but God meant it for good" (Gen. 50:20). The shepherd who leads was led out to die by sinful men; this path to death was God's road to a world of unimaginable good.

This underlying profound belief in the sovereignty of the shepherd and his providential care at every step of the way is why David sings of walking "through" the valley. *Through*. Your valley right now, however its oppressive walls are formed—from depression to death or a thousand other kinds of darkness besides—is not the destination but the journey. For the Lord Jesus, his path was the humiliation of his incarnation and the cross of his atoning death, and then the crown; for us too the road of walking with our shepherd is suffering now, then glory after. But whatever the valley, you are walking *through* it. Jesus is not up ahead asking for directions. He is not lost. He knows where he is leading you. He knows there is a way through it and out of it because that was his own experience of the valley; he has been there ahead of you and for you.

And notice too the little word "walk." If we just pause and think about what we normally do in darkness, I think we will understand why Spurgeon said that every word in verse 4 "has a wealth of meaning."

When our children were much smaller, for some reason the upper floors of our (perfectly safe) house seemed fraught with menace and threat after sundown. Even though by day they lived there happily, by night the creaking floorboards, unoccupied rooms, and shadowy spaces under beds and behind wardrobe doors took on a sinister presence for sensitive little souls. If ever their mother or I asked them to take something upstairs or retrieve something from the top of the house at nighttime, they would stand and look at the stairs and face a choice entirely of their own making. They could either flick the lights on and calmly walk to their destination or keep the dreaded upper floor in darkness and *run* there and back again. This was their mission if they chose to accept it: escape the darkness just in the nick of time, before being lost forever to the monsters of the abyss at the edge of the earth that is number 10 Beechgrove Avenue.

We might smile, of course, at the naivete of their fear and its unnecessary presence in their lives when they are simply going upstairs. But it is a picture of what we are all like with the unknown and what we cannot control.

What kind of person simply *walks* through deepest darkness? Only the person who has no reason to fear it.

I have many privileges as a pastor, nearly all of them involving the array of relationships God has given me within our church family. But none are more awe-inspiring than the encounters I have with sheep who are able to follow their shepherd into the darkness of death. Spurgeon comments:

> "Yea, though I *walk*," as if the believer did not quicken his pace when he came to die, but still calmly *walked* with God. To walk indicates the steady advance of a soul which knows its road, knows its end, resolves to follow the path, feels quite safe, and is therefore perfectly calm and composed.[12]

Seeing the steady advance of a soul unafraid to die is one of the most privileged sights you can have. Such repose comes from knowing that this is the shepherd's path and that this is how he leads. As Spurgeon says, "Many a saint has reaped more joy and knowledge when he came to die than he ever knew when he lived." This comes from the knowledge that the road is a passing through, not a final destination. "Observe that it is not walking *in* the valley, but *through* the valley. We

---

12 Charles Spurgeon, *The Treasury of David*, 3 vols. (Peabody, MA: Hendrickson, 1988), 1:355 (emphasis original).

go through the dark tunnel of death and emerge into the light of immortality."[13]

Psalm 23 is showing us that this safety of the sheep is all-encompassing. We are safe because we know the path we are on is the shepherd's path. This road is simply how he is leading us, and because we are his, we can walk and not run.

But more than this, the sheep's safety comes from the presence of the shepherd and also from the tools of the shepherd. Let's consider those things in turn.

13 Spurgeon, *The Treasury of David*, 1:355 (emphasis original).

5

Where He Is

MY FAMILY AND I regularly fend off grizzly bears.

In our imaginations, that is.

We recently became engrossed in the hit TV series *Alone*. Let me recommend it, if you haven't seen any of this extraordinary experiment in human endurance. The show involves individuals being dropped into a remote location simultaneously but separated from each other, and all given the task of surviving in the wilderness for as long as they can, completely alone. Each one receives a camera on which to record daily life. The environment might be stunningly beautiful, but it is also incredibly unforgiving, with grizzly bears, mountain lions, poisonous plants, and freezing weather the only companions. The person who survives alone for the longest time wins a large cash prize. Of course, you can guess what happens: one by one, in different ways, the competitors succumb to the elements, and the experience becomes too much, the dangerous adventure ends, and they radio in to say they cannot carry on. They are soon rescued and taken home to safety.

Part of my family's enjoyment in watching is our poking fun at one another about who among us would be the least likely to win, for all sorts of reasons. Some of us are scared of flies, for instance, never mind giant bears; some of us are possessed of a sheer inability to not be talking all the time to someone else, unless asleep (and even then we're not always sure the talking stops). We each think we would be the last one standing, and everyone else thinks we wouldn't last one night.

You need to know, however, that the folks taking part in the TV show are first-rate survival experts. I get fed up if I get cold and hungry on a long walk in the park, but the *Alone* participants are not like me. These are people who know how to hunt, trap, kill, start fires, build shelters, insulate against wind and water and ice and snow, and survive against all the odds. And yet—and here is what makes the show so compelling—one by one, slowly, they all begin to unravel because of the sheer brutal effect of being in a dangerous place entirely alone. Some begin to revisit past griefs and talk to the camera about unresolved relational wounds; some even begin to look less and less human as self-care becomes almost impossible and they struggle to find food; all begin to talk openly about their loved ones at home. In the comfort of our living rooms, with our nearest and dearest, we get to observe the chasm that opens up in the human soul as a person grapples with the pitiless existence of being completely and utterly on his or her own.

The show immerses us firsthand in the fact that to be alone—really, truly alone—is one of the greatest hardships a human being can ever bear. A long-running study in loneliness conducted by

Harvard University recently concluded that "loneliness kills. It's as powerful as smoking or alcoholism."[1]

This is why the confession of faith that comes in this middle section of Psalm 23 is so beautiful:

> I will fear no evil,
> for you are with me. (v. 4)

In the next chapter we will see David expand on some concrete elements of the shepherd's presence that put strength into his heart (the rod and the staff in the shepherd's hands), and these too are part of why he is unafraid. But for now, just linger with me in the riches of the simple fact of the shepherd's presence.

It is an astonishing thing to be walking through a valley of deep darkness and to not fear it for the simple reason that you know you do not walk it alone.

Remember that this is one of the three great confessions in Psalm 23 that are its thumping heartbeats—"I shall not want" (v. 1); "I will fear no evil" (v. 4); "I shall dwell in the house of the Lord forever" (v. 6)—and it is at this point, for the very first time in the psalm, that we move from hearing *about* the shepherd to speaking *to* the shepherd. We transition from the third person ("he") to now addressing him directly in the second person ("you"). The meaning of the words, which I think we just intuitively sense, is that it is one thing to be able to say that someone is with me but quite another thing to be able to turn toward that

---

1 Robert Waldinger, cited by Zain Kahn (@heykahn), "Harvard's 84 Year Old Study of Adult Development," Twitter, May 11, 2022, https://twitter.com/heykahn/status /1524422842950975489.

individual and address him personally by saying, "You are with me." If I speak in the third person, it is possible that I have known the benefits of the shepherd by being one sheep among many in the flock, and of course that is precious. But by speaking in the second person, aren't we subtly aware of an intimate deepening of the relationship? It is somehow as if all other sheep are not really in the frame at this moment. The individual relationship that has been presumed and implied all the way through now takes center stage for this central confession of faith to resound so clearly: *this is between you and me, personally, and the deepest comfort I have is that* you *are with* me.

The comfort of the good shepherd's presence is all the more wonderful when we take seriously the reality of the darkness and the presence of evil. It is very important to be clear that David is not saying that the presence of the shepherd removes evil or eradicates darkness, as if being able to say "you are with me" means that the room is now somehow filled with light and happiness. No, the point is that *because* "you are with me," I will not fear the very real darkness and the very real evil I am facing. The comfort is the presence of the shepherd in the midst of the danger rather than the comfort of the removal of the danger.

This is not an insignificant point. Here is one place where, with the greatest respect, we should differ with Charles Spurgeon in some of his comments on this verse. It might preach to say, as Spurgeon does, that shadows cannot bite or kill or destroy, and that for there to be a shadow at all there must be a light, a sun, creating the shadow—and so, "Let us not, therefore, be afraid."[2]

---

2   Charles Spurgeon, *The Treasury of David*, 3 vols. (Peabody, MA: Hendrickson, 1988), 1:355.

But we should notice, of course, that this inverts the meaning of the verse. It is not helpful to deal with the meaning of the metaphor by explaining other things that might be true about the metaphor in general but are clearly at odds with this use in particular. Psalm 23:4 does not counsel that the reason for lack of fear lies in the true nature of shadows; on the contrary, its assumption, I think, is precisely that shadows can be genuinely terrifying places full of grotesque evil, maybe even catastrophic danger, and yet the reason for not fearing is precisely because of who is there with us.

David is not reflecting on the truth about shadows; he is proclaiming the truth about his shepherd. The reason for not fearing resides in who the shepherd is, where and how the shepherd leads, where the shepherd is, what the shepherd holds in his hands, how he welcomes, what he sends, and where he invites. This is the comfort of being in the presence of true strength that is now turned toward me with personal and individual attention to do me good by providing for my every need at every point on my long journey home.

It can do immense damage to frightened sheep to tell them that the presence of the Lord Jesus in their lives should mean the end of danger or the absence of horrifying shadows. John Calvin is a better guide here than Spurgeon. Calvin realizes that the confession "I will fear no evil" actually receives its beauty from the fact that, if left to his own devices, David would be very afraid. It's a lovely point, full of profound understanding of the frailty of the sheep in the valley. Calvin looks ahead to the rest of verse 4 and reasons that if the shepherd's rod and staff "comfort" David, then "what need would he have had of that consolation, if he had not been disquieted and agitated with fear?"[3] Indeed, Calvin goes so far as to suggest the sense must be that David had been "afflicted with fear" but that what he is relaying here is his own personal experience of what it felt like to him to learn to "cast himself on the protection of God."[4] In other words, David has taken his natural fear to God. The picture is of the sheep trembling in the valley with danger on every hand, but then the sheep hears the shepherd's voice and remembers the shepherd's presence and feels the shepherd's tools, and the sheep calms. Only then is it true that the sheep need not fear.

Many of us reading these lines are learning to walk through the valley with our shepherd and to cast ourselves on his protection. My prayer as you work your way through this book, especially if you are currently plunged into deep darkness, is that you will take the time to reflect on who it is that is right beside you wherever you are. As you do so, Psalm 23 will not deny the darkness. "The valley of the shadow of death is a scene of great and uncommon distress—of such trials as overpower the soul; throw it into amazement; break its purposes; fill it with alarm and horror like that which invades trembling nature at the approach of the 'king of terrors.'"[5] Death might be the "king of terrors," but it is a king with many servants who do its bidding ahead of time. It is possible to die a thousand deaths before we die.

3 John Calvin, *Commentary on the Book of Psalms*, trans. James Anderson, vol. 4 (1847; repr., Grand Rapids, MI: Baker, 1998), 395.

4 Calvin, *Commentary on the Book of Psalms*, 4:395.

5 J. M. Mason, cited in William S. Plumer, *Psalms: A Critical and Expository Commentary with Doctrinal and Practical Remarks* (Edinburgh: Banner of Truth, 1975), 313.

In John Bunyan's allegory of the Christian life, *The Pilgrim's Progress*, his depiction of the valley of the shadow of death displays the reality of life as we journey to be with Christ:

> Now this valley was a very solitary place, and as the prophet Jeremiah described it, "a wilderness, a land of deserts, and of pits, a land of drought, and of the shadow of death, a land that no man [but a Christian] passed through, and where no one lived [Jer. 2:6]."
>
> Now here Christian was to be afflicted more than in his fight with Apollyon.[6]

In my own illustrated volume, this is a valley in which, as my friend in the hospital put it, no one is doing forward rolls. In stark contrast—and this might describe where the Lord has led you right now—it is instead a snaking path cut in a ravine with an abyss on either side; the light on the page comes only from the mouth of hell; there are the traps of nets and deadly pitfalls; there is a pile of skulls and mangled bones lying outside a cave.

This is not fanciful or fearmongering on Bunyan's part. It is interesting to note that elsewhere in the Bible the journey from Egypt to the promised land is described as taking place not just in a wilderness land but also

in a land of deserts and pits,
in a land of drought and deep darkness,

6 John Bunyan, *The Pilgrim's Progress: From This World to That Which Is to Come*, ed. C. J. Lovik (Wheaton, IL: Crossway, 2009), 93.

in a land that none passes through,
where no man dwells. (Jer. 2:6)[7]

In Psalm 23:4 once again we are in the metaphorical world of the exodus where the life of faith is conceptualized as a journey to the land of promise through a world of pain. The word for "evil" in verse 4 is open-ended: it "can be used both for moral evil and more generally for things that are not right,"[8] and that is a wonderfully helpful way of seeing our pilgrimage toward the new creation. Whether we are engulfed in the naked evil of others and what they have done to us, or we are simply buffeted to the point of feeling suffocated by the reality of "things that are not right," Psalm 23:4—in its picture of life east of Eden and on this side of the new heavens and the new earth—acknowledges that the darkness we are sometimes in can be intensely real.

And yet, it is precisely *because* of this that what David confesses in verse 4 is so wonderful. In spite of all these things, in the presence of all these things, in the heat of them, he says: "I will fear no evil, *for you are with me.*"

It might help to return to the TV series *Alone*, which I mentioned just a few pages ago. One of the most chilling parts of the show is when the contestants are visited in the night by a deadly animal. In true dramatic fashion, of course, we usually only hear a rustling or a low growl, and the night-vision camera usually only

---

7   Peter C. Craigie, *Psalms 1–50*, Word Biblical Commentary (Grand Rapids, MI: Zondervan, 2004), 207.

8   Richard S. Briggs, *The Lord Is My Shepherd: Psalm 23 for the Life of the Church* (Grand Rapids, MI: Baker Academic, 2021), 96.

shows us the terrified human face inside the tent, but the voice-over tells us about the presence of a grizzly bear or a mountain lion outside, stalking its prey. The unseen nature of the threat heightens the tension and increases our fear.

In these moments, however, my family surprisingly seems only to increase in bravado about what we would each do or how we wouldn't be scared, and what foolproof and obvious steps we would take to ward off the potential attacker. So on one occasion, when we were driving through our city center late at night, I decided to test my children's magnificent courage.

As we drove past a huge but run-down building silhouetted against the skyline—a building we have actually been inside and whose gloomy corridors we know firsthand—I asked my tribe, "Who would go in that building right now and spend the night there all alone?"

Complete silence from the back of the car.

I slowed down, driving along the intimidating shadow line of the edifice's haunting presence. We each stared at it. I raised the stakes. "Who would go in there and spend the night all alone for one million pounds?"

To my amazement, still no answer from the back of the car. All of a sudden my fearless *Alone* devotees turned out to be not so sure about being alone.

Then I asked, "Who would do it for free if I was with you?"

This time a chorus of voices answered in the affirmative! Everyone relaxed, and we were soon back to teasing one another about how we are clearly the most totally useless explorers the world has ever seen (apart from their heroic, bold, intrepid, fearless, valiant, courageous, gallant father).

Isn't this something of the meaning of Psalm 23:4? The shepherd is not just ahead of us, dropping us off at life's scary and deadly destinations, and then keeping a safe distance while we go it alone. The shepherd is not just ahead to lead; he is beside to escort.[9] He has moved from walking in front (Ps. 23:1–3) to coming alongside (v. 4). And having someone with you in the darkness is all that matters isn't it? It changes everything.

As we saw earlier, in Hebrew, the exact middle line of Psalm 23 is the clause "for you are with me." In most English-speaking thought, we tend to put the dominant line at the end of an argument as we build toward a persuasive and definitive climax. But Hebrew thought often works more beautifully by building to a main point in the middle, then throwing further color at the idea by working outward from it again. That is what happens here. The entire psalm centers on this stunning idea that the greatest, strongest, and most gentle and generous shepherd is with us. It is a wonder that we have a shepherd; it is a great wonder that the shepherd we have is "the LORD," the self-existent God, who is faithful to his covenant and whom we have come to know and love in the Lord Jesus Christ—and, wonder of wonders, that shepherd is not far off from us, but *he is with us.*

Martin Luther said that "the Psalter is a little Bible, and the summary of the Old Testament."[10] That's a lovely phrase, for it shows how it's possible to see the whole story of the Bible encapsulated within smaller parts of the Bible. And if Luther was right to say this about the Psalms, then I want to suggest that Psalm 23:4 is itself "a little Bible" within the little Bible of the Psalms

9   Derek Kidner, *Psalms 1–72* (Leicester, UK: Inter-Varsity Press, 1973), 111.
10 Cited in Plumer, *Psalms*, 7.

within the whole Bible. It is a beautiful truth that the message of the whole Bible can be summarized in four simple words: "You are with me."[11]

You are with me.

- In Eden, God lived with Adam and Eve (Gen. 3:8).
- On Mount Horeb, God promised Moses that he would be with him in Egypt (Ex. 3:12).
- At Mount Sinai, God came to live with Israel in a tent, and he spoke with Moses "face to face, as a man speaks to his friend" (Ex. 33:11).
- In the promised land, God came to live with Israel in a temple (1 Kings 8:11).
- In Jesus, God came to live with his people—as Immanuel, "God with us" (John 1:14).
- When Jesus prepared his disciples for his departure, he sent his Holy Spirit so that he could come and live in us (John 14:15–17).
- Jesus promised his disciples, "And behold, I am with you always, to the end of the age" (Matt. 28:20).
- In the new heavens and the new earth, God will once again live with his people. This is how Revelation climactically puts it: "Behold, the dwelling place of God is with man. He will dwell with them, and they will be his people, and God himself will be with them as their God" (Rev. 21:3).

---

11 I owe the thoughts in this and the following paragraphs to Jonathan Gibson's sermon on Ps. 23, "Comfort for All Life," preached at Cambridge Presbyterian Church, February 28, 2016, https://www.cambridgepres.org.uk/.

I hope as you read this you are able to draw deep comfort from the fact that God's presence with his people is the whole Bible in a nutshell. Psalm 23:4 is comforting not for the uniqueness of what it says; rather, we should find it comforting for the beautiful way it manages to say in so few words what the whole Bible says in so many words. You have a shepherd who is with you. The Lord Jesus, your shepherd-king and Savior is with you in your valley, and he will always be with you, for as long as you are there. He will never leave you or forsake you there.

It is my conviction that many believers do not really understand the depth of God's love for them expressed by the fact that, in the Lord Jesus, he is with us. We assume God is with the church in general or with others in the church in particular, but not with me. No, we think, he can't really be with *me*. And as we say this, we cut ourselves off from the whole trajectory of Scripture's story, which is not just that God formed a world and then filled a world but that God himself came to his world, and came to be known in a way as close and personal as a sheep with its shepherd, a traveler with a companion, a guest with a host, a bride with her husband, a servant with its master, even a body with its head. The story of the Bible is that God has come to us in Jesus such that we are able to say to him, "You are with me."

Indeed, this is why in the New Testament the apostle Paul never talks about people being "Christians," as if who we are is a label or title we wear. Instead, Paul speaks about believers being "in Christ," a statement that much better reflects the ultimate truth of our status. Our union with Christ is no less real about us than our sex, nationality, age, height, or any other defining features we may wish to list. Indeed, some of these things can change with time, but our union with Christ does not. He is "with" us because we are "in" him.

As is so often the case, some of our Puritan forebears understood this better than we do. In his wonderful work *The Heart of Christ in Heaven towards Sinners on Earth*, Thomas Goodwin provides a profound meditation on Christ's washing of his disciples' feet and of his Farewell Discourse in the upper room. Goodwin sees the Lord Jesus here condescending to "the laws of bridegrooms"—he reads John's Gospel chapters 13–17 as the outpouring of Christ's heart of love for his disciples with the pleasure and pain of his respective presence and absence the thread that runs through the chapters.[12] Goodwin meditates on these words of Jesus: "And if I go and prepare a place for you, I will come again and will take you to myself, that where I am you may be also" (John 14:3). For Goodwin, Christ is like a husband who first makes everything ready in his father's house and then comes in person to fetch his bride, "and not to send for [her] by others, for it is a time of love." And then Goodwin says, amazingly:

> It is as if he had said, The truth is, I cannot live without you, I shall never be quiet till I have you where I am, that so we may never part again; that is the reason of it. Heaven shall not hold me, nor my Father's company, if I have not you with me, my heart is so set upon you; and if I have any glory, you shall have part of it.[13]

12 Thomas Goodwin, *The Heart of Christ* (Edinburgh: Banner of Truth, 2011), 15.
13 Goodwin, *The Heart of Christ*, 16.

These striking words are Goodwin's attempt to penetrate the stunning reality of John 13–17, chapters which reveal that what the Father, Son, and Spirit share among themselves they have chosen to share with us. Their love for each other is the love they have for us. Their desire to be in each other's presence overflows in the same desire to have us with them in their presence too. In John 17:24 Jesus prays, "Father, I desire that they also, whom you have given me, may be with me where I am." Goodwin's language strains at the very borders of what we can possibly say about how loved we are: "Thou has set my heart upon them, and hast loved them thyself as thou has loved me, and thou hast ordained them to be one in us, even as we are one, and therefore I cannot live long asunder from them; I have thy company, but I must have theirs too; 'I will that they be where I am.'"[14]

So often we disqualify ourselves from Christ's presence, and we think he cannot be with us because we presume his love for us is based on us, on what we are like, on what we have done or not done; but it is not. It is a profound truth, more profound than we realize, that the love of the Father for the Son, and the love of the Son for the Father, is the same love of the Father and the Son for us (John 17:20–26). The fellowship between the persons of the Trinity is a fellowship we are drawn into where the love bestowed on us is a love that already existed without us. We did not create that love or call it forth because of something special in us; no, it was love that already existed without us that we are invited to share in, love given to us, and so the love of

---

14 Goodwin, *The Heart of Christ*, 26.

the Lord Jesus for his disciples displays his very heart toward us in his desire to be with us.

Stunningly, we may say that if the Son wants to be with his Father, then in the same way he also wants to be with his people.

The Lord, your shepherd, is with you.

6

What He Holds

IF YOU SEE A WOMAN in green or blue scrubs with a stethoscope around her neck, you know who she is and what she does.

If a man comes into your house to fix something and he's got a hammer, a saw, a chisel, and a measuring tape on his tool belt hanging round his waist, then you know he's not there to repair your laptop. Who he is and what he does are evident from what he holds.

Psalm 23 teaches us in a beautiful way who the Lord Jesus is and what he does by what he holds. He is heavily armed. This is the further beautiful amplification of why we may not fear the darkest of valleys:

> Your rod and your staff,
> they comfort me. (v. 4)

In the nineteenth century, J. L. Porter met shepherds in the northern Transjordan region, the same part of the world that led

King David to write our psalm. The times have changed, of course, but the ruggedness required to shepherd sheep in that place has remained the same. Here is Porter's description:

> The shepherds themselves had none of that peaceful and placid aspect which is generally associated with pastoral life and habits. They looked like warriors marching to the battlefield—a long gun slung from the shoulder, a dagger and heavy pistols in the belt, a light battle-axe or iron-headed club in the hand. Such were the equipments; and their fierce flashing eyes and scowling countenances showed but too plainly that they were prepared to use their weapons at any moment.[1]

We are so used to the gentleness of Psalm 23 that we may never have felt the steel encased in the velvet. Dale Ralph Davis says:

> Jesus Christ, our Shepherd, is no emaciated weakling. Our Shepherd is a warrior, as shepherds had to be. No one can snatch his sheep out of his hand (John 10:28). The muscles of his arm are flexed to defend his flock; he doesn't carry a club for nothing. He is obviously enough for whatever the valley throws at us.[2]

Spurgeon says that the shepherd's rod and staff lead David to praise him for "the ensigns of [his] sovereignty and of [his]

---

1 This is recounted in Dale Ralph Davis, *Slogging Along in the Paths of Righteousness: Psalms 13–24* (Fearn, Ross-shire, Scotland: Christian Focus, 2014), 168. The description is from J. L. Porter, *Giant Cities of Bashan; and Syria's Holy Places* (New York: T. Nelson, 1867), 46.

2 Davis, *Slogging Along in the Paths*, 168–69.

gracious care."[3] Richard Briggs suggests that "the rod and the staff are the visible symbols of God's invisible presence, in turn suggestive of the shepherd in the valley as the visible symbol of God's presence."[4] Let's consider the sufficiency of the Lord Jesus displayed in what he holds in each hand and see how they bring comfort to his sheep.

First of all, the comfort lies in the distinction between the two items. They are not identical, and their dissimilarity is an important part of the meaning. Kenneth Bailey notes that the word translated "rod" has a semantic range that can include "rod," "scepter," and "weapon," and so a "rod" is not the same thing as a walking stick. "Rather, it is the shepherd's primary offensive weapon for protecting the flock from enemies, be they wild animals or human thieves. The instrument itself is about two and a half feet long with a mace-like end into which the heavy pieces of iron are often embedded. It becomes a formidable weapon."[5] This is why texts like Psalm 2:9 speak of the Lord's anointed one smiting the nations with "a rod of iron" (see also Rev. 2:27; 12:5). The reference is very likely to a wooden item but with iron embedded into it to ensure maximum effectiveness in the hand of the one who wields it. David's own account of his shepherding must surely be referring to an item like a rod as he presents himself to Saul as a combatant able to face mighty Goliath: "Your servant used to keep sheep for his father. And when there came a lion, or a bear, and took a lamb from the

---

3   Charles Spurgeon, *The Treasury of David*, 3 vols. (Peabody, MA: Hendrickson, 1988), 1:356.

4   Richard S. Briggs, *The Lord Is My Shepherd: Psalm 23 for the Life of the Church* (Grand Rapids, MI: Baker Academic, 2021), 101.

5   Kenneth E. Bailey, *The Good Shepherd: A Thousand-Year Journey from Psalm 23 to the New Testament* (London: SPCK, 2015), 50.

flock, I went after him and struck him and delivered it out of his mouth. And if he arose against me, I caught him by his beard and struck him and killed him" (1 Sam. 17:34–35).

At the same time, Bailey makes a good case that the shepherd's rod was not only used for fighting. He draws attention to Leviticus 27:32, where (despite the ESV's rendering of the word as "staff") the shepherd's rod is in view as a counting device for his flock. The idea is that as the sheep reenter the fold at the end of each day, the rod is held up across the entrance to the pen, and the sheep are counted in as they pass beneath it. (Today we would use a digital sign-up form or a scannable QR code for check-in to the premises.) This is the shepherd's way of personally checking that his sheep are all present and accounted for. "Thus the sheep (in the flock of God) can note the shepherd's rod and remember that it is an 'alarm system' used to assure everyone's safety. If any sheep is lost, the shepherd will be alerted during the 'evening count.'"[6] This is a beautiful picture, for the implement of warfare is now turned to a different use. The protection here lies not in an instrument of aggression but in a symbol of loving possession. The rod in the shepherd's hand performs both these roles; so what is the comfort for us here in the valley?

The rod helps us to know, as John Goldingay says, that having the Lord "with" us "is not merely a feeling. It does not signify mere presence but also action. . . . This presence expresses itself by aggressive action to defeat enemies and thus protect the one to whom Yhwh is committed."[7]

6   Bailey, *The Good Shepherd*, 51.
7   John Goldingay, *Psalms*, vol. 1, *Psalms 1–41* (Grand Rapids, MI: Baker Academic, 2006), 351.

Defeating enemies and protecting sheep: both of these are present in the shepherding work of the Lord Jesus for us. "My sheep hear my voice and I know them, and they follow me. I give them eternal life, and they will never perish, and no one will snatch them out of my hand" (John 10:28). Such language implies, of course, that some will attempt to snatch, that there are forces out there who seek to do sheep harm, and yet we are encased in the shepherd's strong hand, which is in turn grasped in the Father's strong hand (John 10:29). This ready willingness to protect his sheep follows from the fact that Jesus knows exactly who belongs to him. He "calls his own sheep by name and leads them out. When he has brought out all his own, he goes before them, and the sheep follow him, for they know his voice" (John 10:3–4). Numbered by Jesus, we are led by Jesus; led by Jesus, we are protected by Jesus; and protected by Jesus, we are comforted by Jesus.

Some of us reading these lines feel very weak. The circumstances of life have pressed us down, and we feel pretty broken. This shepherd, God's servant, will not break a bruised reed or snuff out a smoldering wick (Matt. 12:20, citing Isa. 42:3); he is tender to all our brokenness. But this same Jesus "will faithfully bring forth justice" (Isa. 42:3; Matt. 12:20). So let the rod in Jesus's hand also put strength into your failing heart; for, remember, he is leading you through the valley, and on the other side is the house of the Lord where we will dwell forever. We should always remember how the Bible ends: on the other side of it all the Lamb wins. The Lamb wins because he is also a Lion. We should never mistake the tenderness of our shepherd for weakness, or his care for us for carelessness about all that threatens us.

This point can really come alive to us when we consider how we experience this sort of shepherding in everyday life. Several years ago, I went to stay with the younger of my two brothers in his flat in Newcastle, England. It was a weekend to remember as I was introduced to Sean, my brother's Neapolitan Mastiff–Bullmastiff dog, who had also come from Great Dane stock (and surely every other breed of huge canine, maybe even horse). To this day I have never seen another dog as magnificent as Sean. Completely docile in my brother's presence, he was a threat to all the world beyond. You did not look Sean in the eye; you did not mess with Sean; you gave Sean whatever he wanted whenever he wanted it, and you could be sure of one thing: walking down the street with Sean, my brother and I too could get whatever we wanted—or so it seemed. Crowds parted. Grown men protectively put their arms in front of women and children and held them back against the walls of narrow spaces as Sean and his two-man entourage passed through. It was magnificent. Sean was with us.

I remember nighttime as I slept and Sean lay a few meters from me by the front door. I was awakened on more than one occasion by his low, deep-throated rumbling growl as people passed by outside. These folks making their way home were just a little too close for Sean's liking, but they were innocently unaware of the guardian they would meet in a terrible way should any of them come through the door as a foe. I smiled a few times as I drifted back to sleep almost wishing someone would attempt a break-in they would never forget. Or ever be able to repeat.

So big, so strong, so powerful: for one night, I had a shepherd. There was nothing to fear.

David knows he has no less security in his shepherd. He speaks to him personally, "I will fear no evil for your rod is in your hand to comfort me," and that is what you and I can say to the Lord Jesus. He brooks no rival, and he has no peer for the zeal of his jealous love for his people. Our shepherd will not abandon his sheep.

But a rod is not the only thing in Jesus's hands: he also holds a staff. If a rod was a cudgel to deter, the staff was used to direct, to round up the sheep and to pull them in. One instrument for defense, the other for correction. The staff was the shepherd's equivalent to a lead for a dog; something used to train and guide the sheep, to keep the sheep near and on the right path, going in the right direction. The word for "staff" is related to a verb meaning "press down" and "lean on," something that the shepherd does as he walks or climbs and as he directs his sheep. "The shepherd's staff is not for defending the flock from external threat, but for caring for the sheep as he leads them daily in search of food, drink, tranquillity and rest."[8] This additional shepherding tool shows us that we need both things: defense and discipline, protection and provision. It is a picture of the entire and absolute responsibility that the shepherd takes for his sheep. In this comprehensiveness, there is challenge and there is comfort.

Many commentators point out that the word "comfort" in Psalm 23 suggests both "emotional encouragement and sometimes action that changes a situation, and both would be relevant in this context."[9] Once again the psalm links with the language of an exodus where God tells the prophet Isaiah, "Comfort, comfort, my people" because a new exodus is coming in the return

8   Bailey, *The Good Shepherd*, 53.
9   Goldingay, *Psalms*, 1:351.

from exile (Isa. 40–55). God's comfort is not sent on a Hallmark card; it is God himself using his own strong arm to redeem and rescue his people. This is what he does with his rod and staff in our lives. We need to hear this, and we need both tools.

Some of us want Jesus to protect us from our enemies with his rod, but we don't want Jesus to protect us from ourselves with his staff. We like the idea of Jesus coming down hard on others; we are less enamored when he reaches us personally and directs us somewhere we don't want to go. But what is my greatest enemy right now as I type these lines? It is my own sinful heart. My love of myself, my self-pity, my distorted belief that the grass might be greener somewhere else, or my deeply twisted, subtle belief that the path of righteousness might not be the path of happiness. "Prone to wander, Lord, I feel it, / prone to leave the God I love," the hymn says.[10] Oh how I need Christ's staff in my life to continually pull me back to him.

Some of us have wandered off the shepherd's paths of righteousness, and we are grazing in fields we know we should never have visited. If we're honest, we're kind of wondering how we got there. It might be that we're in a relationship we know we shouldn't be in, or we're thinking about getting into one we know we shouldn't be thinking about. Whatever the specifics, we can just sense that a new distance has opened between us and the shepherd, and between us and other sheep, and it's all because we have been slowly but surely putting ourselves beyond the reach of his staff.

10 Robert Robinson, "Come, Thou Fount of Every Blessing" (1758), https://hymnary.org/.

It might be that we are not reading our Bibles as much as we used to, or we are not in church as much as we used to be. For some time now we've grown cool in speaking to others about the Lord because we've felt a creeping embarrassment in doing so. Maybe we are not listening to the loving rebukes or advice of our Christian friends like we did before. We are ducking and diving to keep ourselves out of the reach of the hook of the shepherd's staff. Maybe we still like being associated with a particular church and a group of sheep with whom we are familiar. We haven't left yet, but we're just beginning to wander out of reach. The rod and the staff are not comforting us.

Some people are surprised to discover that the elders of a church hold both the rod and the staff in their hands. It's why elders meet together—not just to pray and plan but also to pastor the flock, and sometimes that work is painful, heartbreaking, and difficult as shepherds work to pull back straying sheep. I've come to learn that sometimes the same sheep who like the idea of elders fending off the wolves with a rod by keeping false teaching out of the church get quite a surprise when they feel the shepherd's staff on their shoulder as they are gently, lovingly sought because they haven't been in church much themselves recently. Shepherds with rods and staffs in hand don't belong in meetings pushing paper. They are with sheep in coffee shops and living rooms and hospital bedsides; they shepherd in graveyards and crematoria and in the counseling room; they hold out bread and wine at a table and pour water from a font or in a tank or a river. Shepherds ask one another where they are with the Lord right now, and they ask sheep where they are with the Lord today. They love his staff in their lives and in the lives of their flock.

Maybe this psalm is working like a reset button for your life as you read. Maybe it's time to click refresh on the home screen of your life and start over.

Maybe it's time to come home.

Maybe it's time to look up and see how far you've wandered but, as you do so, to see the shepherd who is waiting to walk with you again.

Maybe it's time to speak to someone.

Or maybe it's simply time to keep looking ahead and to carry on walking with Jesus as you have been doing for more years than you can count.

I believe that the sense we have of whether our souls are being daily restored by the Lord Jesus (Ps. 23:2) will be directly proportional to our felt need to be in our shepherd's presence and to spend time with him. If we do not think we need him, we will not be restored by him. It is the same here: the fear we feel in the valley will be directly proportional to our need to be in his presence. If we do not sense our need for him, we will be going it alone in the darkness. But our coming in and going out with him, our easy familiarity with him and his word and his people and his means of grace in preaching, praying, receiving the Lord's Supper and celebrating baptism, these are the ways in which his rod and his staff will offer to our souls the most profound comfort.

The more distance we create between us and these means of grace, these tokens of the shepherd's strong and gracious presence, the more fear there will be in the valley.

———

The Lord's my shepherd, I'll not want.
He makes me down to lie
in pastures green: he leadeth me
the quiet waters by.

My soul he doth restore again;
and me to walk doth make
within the paths of righteousness,
ev'n for his own name's sake.

Yea, though I walk through death's dark vale,
yet will I fear no ill:
for thou art with me; and thy rod
and staff me comfort still.

My table thou hast furnishèd
in presence of my foes;
my head with oil thou dost anoint,
and my cup overflows.

Goodness and mercy all my life
shall surely follow me:
and in God's house for evermore
my dwelling-place shall be.

WILLIAM WHITTINGHAM ET AL. (1650)

based on Psalm 23

PART 3

————————

THE GUEST AND
THE HOST

You prepare a table before me
    in the presence of my enemies;
you anoint my head with oil;
    my cup overflows.
Surely goodness and mercy shall follow me
    all the days of my life,
and I shall dwell in the house of the Lord
    forever.

PSALM 23:5–6

C. S. LEWIS UNDERSTOOD Psalm 23 better than he knew.

It may surprise you to hear that Lewis was unable to reconcile the beauty of verses 1–4 of Psalm 23 with what he regarded as a spirit of hatred in verse 5, a spirit "almost comic in its naivety."

For Lewis, the notion that a host might treat his guest to a feast while his enemies are made to look on is irretrievably spiteful. "The poet's enjoyment of his present prosperity would not be complete unless those horrid enemies (who used to look down their noses at him) were watching it all and hating it. . . . The pettiness and vulgarity of it, especially in such surroundings, are hard to endure."[1]

Yet, for all this, I have a favorite scene in Lewis's *The Lion, the Witch and the Wardrobe* that never fails to make me smile because it expresses the true meaning of Psalm 23:5 so beautifully.

Around the halfway mark in *The Lion, the Witch and the Wardrobe*, Lewis give us two chapters: "The Spell Begins to Break" and "Aslan Is Nearer." At this point in the fable, the white witch's power is waning, the frozen wastelands of Narnia are thawing, winter is retreating, and Christmas is returning. In a land where it was always winter and never Christmas, beautiful things are now reemerging: Father Christmas is back, there are presents and gifts, and with Aslan nearer and on the move, we know we are heading for a showdown with the white witch. As she is racing to the stone table, she stumbles across this scene:

---

1   C. S. Lewis, *Reflections on the Psalms* (London: Fontana, 1961), 23–24. The same idea is present in different form in Harold S. Kushner, *The Lord Is My Shepherd: Healing Wisdom of the Twenty-Third Psalm* (New York: Knopf, 2003), 125–34.

. . . a merry party, a squirrel and his wife with their children and two satyrs and a dwarf and an old dog-fox, all on stools around a table. Edmund couldn't quite see what they were eating, but it smelled lovely and there seemed to be decorations of holly and he wasn't at all sure that he didn't see something like plum pudding.[2]

As the white witch arrives at the feast, she recoils in outrage and horror:

"What is the meaning of this?" asked the Witch Queen. Nobody answered.

"Speak vermin!" she said again. . . . "What is the meaning of all this gluttony, this waste, this self-indulgence? Where did you get all these things?"[3]

C. S. Lewis wrote better than he knew.

You prepare a table before me
in the presence of my enemies;
you anoint my head with oil;
my cup overflows. (Ps. 23:5)

This strange little episode in The Chronicles of Narnia goes unnoticed so often, and yet it adds a wonderful element to the story. For in an allusive and understated way, it manages to suggest that,

2 C. S. Lewis, *The Lion, the Witch and the Wardrobe* (1950; repr., London: HarperCollins, 1980), 105.

3 Lewis, *The Lion, the Witch and the Wardrobe*, 105–6.

when all is said and done, the point of everything is not warfare and the clash of good and evil but fellowship and feasting. In a world made new there is overflowing joy in the delightful gifts of the King and in the lavish goodness of his reign.

In this final section of the book we are nearing the end of our journey with the shepherd. All the way through the psalm, the sheep are out there in the world, in the wild, and are following the shepherd, being restored and comforted by him, but the end goal is always to have the sheep safely in the fold at close of day. In these final verses of Psalm 23 we come to its third glorious confession of faith. Here is what the Lord Jesus will do for us:

I shall dwell in the house of the LORD
  forever. (v. 6)

From this vantage point we can look back over the journey: "The green pastures may be the normal place, the valley of the shadow of death the fearful place, in front of the enemies the dangerous place, and the house of the LORD the abiding place."[4]

In every place, at every season of life, the shepherd is with us, and there is more to savor here of his delightful presence as he leads us home.

---

4 Dale Ralph Davis, *Slogging Along in the Paths of Righteousness: Psalms 13–24* (Fearn, Ross-shire, Scotland: Christian Focus, 2014), 173.

7

How He Welcomes

WHEN WE ARE CLOSE to the Lord Jesus—in the same way that David is close to his shepherd in Psalm 23—then there are many different facets to our relationship with him.

It is well observed by commentators that in verses 5–6 of the psalm the imagery changes from that of sheep and shepherd to that of guest and host. We move now from pictures of pastures and waters, and rod and staff, to oil on the head and cup in the hand. It is as if David addresses the Lord as his shepherd and praises him: "Your care for me is so comprehensive, so absolute, that, more than the way a loving shepherd treats a precious sheep, you treat me the way a lavish host treats a special guest." That this is a picture of total care is why we shouldn't think of it as a transition that leaves off the idea of the Lord as our shepherd; rather this is *how* he shepherds. It is a way of saying that there are no limits to what he does for us—it extends even this far.[1]

---

1 See Richard S. Briggs, *The Lord Is My Shepherd: Psalm 23 for the Life of the Church* (Grand Rapids, MI: Baker Academic, 2021), 102; Peter C. Craigie, *Psalms 1–50*, Word Biblical Commentary (Grand Rapids, MI: Zondervan, 2004), 207.

This part of the psalm is where, perhaps more than any other, some commentators lose themselves in the speculative details of what individual words and the whole picture might actually be referencing. In contrast, I want to suggest that all the discrete parts of verse 5 are best understood in light of the overall atmosphere they combine to create. This cumulative sense of the whole can let us lay out the details quite simply to see how they are full of very rich meaning.

The most important word in the title of this chapter is "How." That is the aroma of Psalm 23:5. Yes, we are entering a new domain, shifting from the idea of care for the animal world to care prepared for humans, but do not move so quickly that you fail to notice *how* this host is operating. Look at the *way* he does it.

Notice immediately that we remain so comfortably in the realm of second-person address: "*You* prepare a table before me." Perhaps, like me, you have been present at some exquisite function that was a delight to attend, but you did not meet the host, nor were you able to speak to him or her personally. Perhaps the host was too busy or too important, or your association with him or her too distant because you were at the event only through a tenuous second- or third-hand connection. You benefitted from the host's generosity and enjoyed what the table offered, but you did not know the host and he or she certainly did not come looking for you.

I hope by now it is evident how Psalm 23:5 is so different from this in what it holds out to us during our journey with our shepherd through our exodus wilderness. He hosts us personally and we can know him personally. It is as if, in all David's speech about his shepherd in Psalm 23, what he's saying is so wonderful that, by the time he gets to verse 4, he turns from speaking *about* the Lord to speaking *to* the Lord himself—face on, as it were—and addresses him directly:

> I will fear no evil
> for you are with me.

And it just continues—he now can't stop as the language of praise flows out of him:

> You prepare a table before me . . .
> you anoint my head with oil. (v. 5)

What is said is beautiful, of course, but it is delivered in the direct address and close intimacy of personal relationship.

One of my prayers as I write these lines is that, when reading this book, you say the word "you" to the Lord Jesus many times. Yes, this is a book about our shepherd, companion, and host, but it is my own feeble attempt to lead us to worship him for being all these things for us—and worship always turns from third-person description to second-person adoration. Sunday by Sunday at Trinity Church in Aberdeen, one of my prayers is that we are never long into our gathered worship before each person in the room is saying "you" to God: in their hearts or out loud, addressing him personally as Creator, Father, Master, Savior, Shepherd, King, Friend, and Judge. When you don't know someone or you're out of relationship with someone, you only talk about "him" or "her." But when you know and love and want to be with someone, you say "you."

Where are you with him?

Let's go deeper into it by moving from the pronouns to the verbs. There are three verbs here, with two of them describing the explicit activity of the host and the third making his activity implicit: "you *prepare* a table," "you *anoint* my head," and "my cup *overflows*," the sense being that he fills my cup to overflowing. The host is active and I am passive; he is the one giving so much and I am the one receiving all that he gives. Every detail is lovely. Purely because of our host's benevolence, we have moved from threat in verse 4 to triumph in verse 5, and we find ourselves, in Derek Kidner's words, at a "well-set table," our bodies perfumed with "festive oil," and our hands holding a "brimming cup."[2]

The word for "prepare" is used in the Old Testament for setting things out in order. The occasion could be anything from a feast, like here, to a case at law (Ps. 50:21), but the word was particularly used to describe the priestly ministry of "laying the altar fire and arranging the pieces of the burnt offering (Leviticus 1:6ff)," notes Kidner.[3] This is to say, the word describes exactness of care and attention to detail—and these are always the marks of the very best of hosts.

A friend once visited us for the evening. He had come at our request—he was helping me with a painful pastoral situation—and he had traveled some distance to be with us. Somehow that evening, however, we got our wires crossed in a very embarrassing way. We thought we were hosting him for coffee and a conversation; he thought the invitation included food, and he

2 Derek Kidner, *Psalms 1–72* (Leicester, UK: Inter-Varsity Press, 1973), 111–12.
3 Kidner, *Psalms 1–72*, 58.

arrived at our home on an empty stomach. Eventually, our poor guest couldn't help himself any longer and, out of sheer hunger, confessed that he hadn't eaten because he thought we were going to share an evening meal together! You can imagine the embarrassment all around and the scrambling through the larder and the red-faced excuses and apologies and the very real sense that, albeit unwittingly, we had failed as hosts for our guest. We were completely unprepared.

W. S. Plumer observes that "to prepare a table was to make ready a feast. It was to do more than to give a loaf of bread to a weary pilgrim. It was to detain one as a guest and set before him the best of everything that could under the circumstances be had."[4] I love the idea of "detaining" someone in order to treat him as a guest. We so often use that term in a negative way: usually we detain in order to punish or restrict and to visit bad things upon someone. But Plumer has captured the sense of Psalm 23:5: the Lord is making us stop where we are, and he is holding us back a while, detaining us, specifically so that he can surprise us with the full extent of his very best care. Calvin says the idea of God preparing a table for David "means that God furnished him with sustenance without trouble or difficulty on his part, just as if a father should stretch forth his hand to give food to his child."[5]

Consider too the head anointed with oil and the cup filled to overflowing. Just like we would take visitors' coats on their arrival

4   William S. Plumer, *Psalms: A Critical and Expository Commentary with Doctrinal and Practical Remarks* (Edinburgh: Banner of Truth, 1975), 314.

5   John Calvin, *Commentary on the Book of Psalms*, trans. James Anderson, vol. 4 (1847; repr., Grand Rapids, MI: Baker, 1998), 396.

in our homes, in David's culture you would wash their feet and perfume their heads with oil. Just like we would never leave a guest thirsty, staring at an empty glass and wondering if there'll ever be a refill, so too this host ensures that the cup of his guests never runs dry. The word for "anoint" here is not the word used frequently throughout the Old Testament for the ritual anointing of kings or priests; rather the more literal sense of the word is "being or growing fat."[6] A translation might say, "You make my head fat with the oil."[7] Although this might sound strange to us, the sense is simply of the liberality of the host; the provision is lavish and rich, not meager or minimal. Anointing is a gesture of hospitality, and it is generous, which is why the cup overflows. To speak about "my cup" is to refer to "the psalmist's experience of life."[8] David is saying here that the blessings of the Lord have flowed freely into every part of his existence such that on every hand he sees the Lord's bounty toward him personally.

Kenneth Bailey's study of Psalm 23 is a delight to read at this point, not simply because of his understanding of hospitality in Middle Eastern culture, but also because it shines a light on what such language displays about the nature of God. Bailey cites the work of George Lamsa:

> In the East, a man's fame is spread by means of his table and lavish hospitality rather than by his possessions. Strangers and neighbours alike discuss tables where they have been guests.

6   Briggs, *The Lord Is My Shepherd*, 108.
7   James M. Hamilton, *Psalms*, vol. 1, Evangelical Biblical Theology Commentary (Bellingham, WA: Lexham, 2021), 297.
8   Craigie, *Psalms 1–50*, 208.

Such tales spread from one town to another and are handed down from one generation to another. There is considerable gossip as to how guests and strangers are entertained.[9]

In traditional Middle East society the "master of the house *provides* the food, he does not *prepare* it."[10] Abraham the host orders food to be prepared for his guests (Gen. 18:1–8); the father in the parable of the prodigal son orders a banquet to be prepared (Luke 15:22–23). The host does not prepare the feast himself.

How astonishing it is, then, that this psalm should be clothing the Lord of the burning bush—the great "I am," who has no need of anyone or anything—in the language of a host who is lavish beyond compare to those who have such need. The greatest of hosts himself prepares the most lavish of feasts for the lowliest of creatures. How amazing it is that the Lord of heaven should be seen here spreading his fame in all the earth by wanting to be known as a certain kind of host. This is a facet to his display of his own glory, the Lord doing everything "for his name's sake" (Ps. 23:3), which we often overlook because we associate God's glory and fame with his strength and salvation more than we do with his individual attention to those he has redeemed. But it is in God's nature to serve us as much as it is to save us.

You know—you just know—when you have been with good hosts. Wouldn't you agree? It's impossible to miss. The little

---

9   Kenneth E. Bailey, *The Good Shepherd: A Thousand-Year Journey from Psalm 23 to the New Testament* (London: SPCK, 2015), 54. Bailey is citing George Lamsa, *The Shepherd of All: The Twenty-Third Psalm* (Philadelphia: Holman, 1930), 65–66.

10   Bailey, *The Good Shepherd*, 55 (emphasis original).

touches, the attention to detail, the comprehensiveness of the care. Psalm 23 is a portrait of just such a host.

Do you know how God welcomes you? Do you know just how good the Lord Jesus is in his care of you, his guest? His welcome is second to none.

Some of us reading these pages have an ingrained belief that we are largely irrelevant to God. We have messed up, screwed up, dropped out, or maybe burned out, and we just haven't quite seen yet that with this shepherd and this host there is the kind of welcome that we've never seen before. Is the Lord miserly or magnificent?

Pause and ask yourself: In my mind's eye, what is God like? Do I think of him as being like the Grinch, or is he like Father Christmas? I think this is why C. S. Lewis paints Father Christmas into *The Lion, the Witch and the Wardrobe.* With Aslan safely installed as the Christ figure in the stories, it is as if Lewis just can't help but to include Father Christmas as well. When Aslan is overturning the curse and winter is becoming spring, well *of course* it's going to be Christmas and *of course* there are going to be gifts.

What is God like to you? Is he like the most generous of fathers, who lays the stocking on your bed or fills it over the fireplace while you sleep, so that you wake to a wonderful world of generous bounty and to presents round the tree in a house crammed to overflowing with good things? Or is God like the head teacher with his rule book in hand and his watching eye ready to catch you at your next misdemeanor?

Some Christians I meet are miserly. They don't give their money properly, or their time or any other resources; they give nothing like what they could or should do. The simple reason they don't is that they are not like God in how he gives, and the reason they are not like him is that they haven't properly seen him for who he truly is. A rod and staff in his hands—yes, sure, of course. But perfume and wine? Surely there must be some mistake.

It is a fact of life that our reputation precedes us in the way we give and the way we welcome. It might come as a surprise to you, but I can guarantee that the people you rub shoulders with every day will have an impression of you as either tight or generous. Maybe most of us would be surprised if we knew what others thought of us in this regard. Many of us think of ourselves with liberality of heart while others only ever experience from our hand the bare minimum.

All of this is a challenge to our tightfistedness when we reflect afresh on how openhanded the Lord Jesus is, and how he is this to me personally, of all people. Jesus knew that people were sizing him up all the time based on his table fellowship. "The Son of Man has come eating and drinking, and you say, 'Look at him! A glutton and a drunkard, a friend of tax collectors and sinners!'" (Luke 7:34). That makes Jesus your friend today; it makes him my friend, the kind of friend who welcomes sinners. Jesus ate with sinners, and he still does. Every time we share bread and wine together around his table, we remember the astonishing wonder that the Master of the house eats and drinks with the servants of the house, and that he laid down his life for us and calls us his friends. Each meal in the wilderness is a foretaste of the banquet to come: "Blessed are those servants whom the master finds awake when he comes. Truly, I say to you, he will dress himself for service and have them recline at table, and he will come and serve them"

(Luke 12:37). More wine? A second helping? One day Jesus will ask you personally.

These stunning actions of Jesus our host help us, I think, with some of the other details in Psalm 23:5:

> You prepare a table before me
> in the presence of my enemies.

A lot of commentators have spilt a lot of ink on the question of what this "table" might be, who these "enemies" are, and what it says about the Lord that he would prepare a feast in their presence. Some suggest that the table is literally the high plateau of a mountain range, like Tabletop Mountain in South Africa, so the idea is that the shepherd has led the sheep up there to feed in full view of predators and yet he protects them.[11] Some suggest that the table is the raised wooden table, like a modern-day feeding trough, on which some shepherds fed their sheep because of the enemies of parasites on the ground.[12] Others (I think much more plausibly) point to 2 Samuel 17:27–29, where David is on the run from Absalom and he is literally fed by soldiers while he is being hunted.[13] The same debate applies to "the enemies" in the verse; there are many ideas out there about who they might have been.

---

11 W. Phillip Keller, *A Shepherd Looks at Psalm 23* (Grand Rapids, MI: Zondervan, 1970), 91–99.

12 J. Douglas MacMillan, *The Lord Our Shepherd* (Leyland, UK: Evangelical Press of Wales, 1983), 115–18.

13 Alec Motyer, *New Bible Commentary* (Leicester, UK: Inter-Varsity Press, 1994), 500–501; Dale Ralph Davis, *Slogging Along in the Paths of Righteousness: Psalms 13–24* (Fearn, Ross-shire, Scotland: Christian Focus, 2014), 169.

We can actually receive a measure of help from the lack of specificity in the text. The open-endedness aids us. Sometimes the Bible is like that. We simply do not know, for instance, what the apostle Paul's "thorn in the flesh" was (2 Cor. 12:7), and that is a very good thing. For it stops us from limiting the applications of the sufficiency of God's grace and his power made perfect in weakness (2 Cor. 12:9) to Paul's specific affliction. It allows us to benefit from this text in a number of different connections. God has his ways of keeping people humble who might otherwise be proud, and he has many different means of making people weak to display his strength.

So it is, here. Just like there are things in this life that can almost break you (2 Cor. 12), so too there are many different enemies of Christ and his flock in this world (Ps. 23). There are wolves, thieves, and persecutors; there is the world itself, the flesh, and the devil. The point of it all is that when enemies are against you, Jesus is for you and with you. When all others forsake us, Jesus welcomes us, cares for us, protects us, and feeds us.

Indeed, it is far more helpful to us to see what these things meant in Jesus's day and in his own life and ministry. Once again, we should read the language of Psalm 23:5 as an exodus echo that gets louder and clearer in Jesus's ministry so that we see the full beauty of the verse's meaning in his light. In Psalm 78 we read of the Israelites' rebellion against God in the desert:

They tested God in their heart
   by demanding the food they craved.
They spoke against God, saying,
   "Can God spread a table in the wilderness?" (vv. 18–19)

This means that we don't need to know the details of David's situation in Psalm 23 to know he is telling exodus-shaped stories about God's covenant faithfulness and constant provision to his rebellious and wayward people. When the Lord rescues and redeems, his sheep rebel. When he provides and feeds, his sheep grumble and doubt. This psalm is David's own expression of going against the wilderness grain; it is his affectionate love for his shepherd-host confessing that, contrary to the natural tendency of the selfish sheep, David is learning that God can in fact always be trusted.

We have already seen how in Mark's Gospel Jesus feeds hungry people in a desolate place, but he does so in the face of doubt and disbelief about his capacity to meet their needs (Mark 6:34–37). The same thing happens again in Mark 8: "And his disciples answered him, 'How can one feed these people with bread here in this desolate place?'" (Mark 8:4). Those words are almost a direct echo of Psalm 78:19. Jesus is the host who has come to lead his people home by feeding them, but they do not recognize who he is or what he can give.

And more than this, Jesus does it all in the presence of his enemies. Remember Herod lurking in the background in Mark 6 with the implicit threat that what happened to John the Baptist will happen to all who preach the same message he did? Kenneth Bailey points out how much of Jesus's eating and drinking in the Gospels happens in the presence of those who are either criticizing him for his choice of culinary companions or even coming to view his dining habits with murderous eyes.[14] "And when they saw it, they all grumbled, 'He has gone in to be the guest of a

---

14 Bailey, *The Good Shepherd*, 57–58.

man who is a sinner'" (Luke 19:7). As the table is spread, so the cross begins to loom.

All of this helps with the unfortunate interpretation of Psalm 23:5 provided by C. S. Lewis. Recall that for Lewis there is a "pettiness and vulgarity" to the idea that one might enjoy a feast in the presence of enemies; he even goes so far as to call psalms with such ideas "terrible or (dare we say?) contemptible."[15] On the one hand, it is important to observe that Lewis's reading actually projects into the verse the idea that conflict between the guest or host and the enemies is a thing of the past, so that in the feasting the enemy is humiliated by triumphant vindictiveness. But, of course, Psalm 23:5 says nothing of this. What if the conflict is actually ongoing? What if the conflict is coming to a climax? What if the guest is, in fact, in great danger from his enemies as he eats, but he eats to woo and win them, not to belittle or degrade?

On the other hand, the forcefulness of Lewis's reading really melts away when we see the Lord Jesus eating and drinking in the presence of his enemies. He is not humiliating them; he is seeking to humble them, and in so doing he shows his own humility. He is not gloating over them; he is inviting them. "For the Son of Man came to seek and to save the lost" (Luke 19:10). The door is open to all. There is a ready, wide, capacious invitation to any who will come and eat and drink with him. All you need to do is know that you are lost.

So the table is spread in the presence of his enemies, but it is precisely that—a table. It is not a bar of justice in their presence;

---

15 C. S. Lewis, *Reflections on the Psalms* (London: Fontana, 1961), 24.

not yet anyway. It is not a sword. Not yet. It is a table, where Jesus is defining the people of God as those who will recognize him as the true shepherd of Israel, the good shepherd, the now-present-with-us Immanuel-host of the messianic banquet long promised in the prophets and so passionately anticipated by God's people. A table, with food and drink, is where covenants can be sealed and fellowship formed, it is where relationships can be restored and enemies reconciled as friends, and it is where so many choose to seal their own fate in their rejection of Jesus. Judas went out into the night, but he went out with clean feet and with bread and wine in his belly. He left a table that a loving host had prepared in the presence of his murderous enemies.

Let me finish this chapter by simply going back to its opening words and asking if you can now feel the atmosphere of Psalm 23:5 in *how* the Lord Jesus welcomes. He has displayed his complete and total sufficiency for all our needs and his lavish love for the most wayward prodigal or most vile outcast. His enemies are not defined as people who have done bad things, and his friends are not defined as those who have done good things. No, his enemies are those who cannot bear the fact that he eats with people who have done bad things. People like me, and you.

His welcome is vast and free; it is sealed in blood and it is offered in bread and wine. It is an ocean of generosity in a world of stymied and miserly quid-pro-quo reciprocity. In Bailey's words, this is "costly love." He suggests that the core meaning of "a table in the presence of my enemies" is this: that Jesus "demonstrates costly love to me irrespective of who is watching. People hostile to me will observe what he is doing and he knows that their hostility against me will be extended to him as a result. He doesn't care. He offers that love anyway."[16]

This is why some commentators are right, I believe, to see, in the language of the cup overflowing not just that the host keeps on giving to me but also a sense of what it feels like to be the one receiving such a munificent cup. If to speak of an overflowing cup is a way of describing bountiful provision, then Psalm 23:5 also expresses how life with this host is "full of blessing, overflowing with thanksgiving."[17] In other words, the atmosphere of the verse is as much gratitude as it is generosity—better, it breathes the kind of great gratitude that is born of great generosity.

Like almost nothing else, your gratitude for Jesus will be the measure of where you are with him. Those who have been forgiven little, love little. Those forgiven much, love much (Luke 7:36–50).

As Harold Kushner puts it, "For those who have cultivated the habit of gratitude, no matter how large a bowl we set out to receive God's blessings, it will always overflow."[18]

Spurgeon is even better. A poor cottager broke a piece of bread and filled a glass with cold water, and as she did so, she asked, "What, all this, and Jesus Christ too?"[19]

16 Bailey, *The Good Shepherd*, 57.
17 Craigie, *Psalms 1–50*, 208.
18 Harold S. Kushner, *The Lord Is My Shepherd: Healing Wisdom of the Twenty-Third Psalm* (New York: Knopf, 2003), 155.
19 Charles Spurgeon, *The Treasury of David*, 3 vols. (Peabody, MA: Hendrickson, 1988), 1:356.

8

What He Sends

THE TITLE OF THIS CHAPTER might seem a little strange, for Psalm 23:6 speaks about two things "following" us: goodness and mercy. So why are we thinking about *sending* here?

Almost without exception, commentators on this verse point out that the verb "follow" is in fact a very weak rendering. Richard Briggs goes so far as to say that it is "the one word in the whole psalm that in my opinion has been persistently poorly translated in English."[1] Instead, at the very heart of the word is the meaning "pursue." Goodness and mercy pursue David; they do not merely follow him. The word is so intensive, it is often used in combat scenes, where people are "pursued" to death, but the word itself is not negative and can be used in delightfully positive, instructive ways:

Turn away from evil and do good;
    seek peace and pursue it. (Ps. 34:14)

---

1   Richard S. Briggs, *The Lord Is My Shepherd: Psalm 23 for the Life of the Church* (Grand Rapids, MI: Baker Academic, 2021), 115.

In Psalm 23:6, says Briggs, "It is almost as if the verse attributes both agency and initiative to these divine characteristics here, whereas 'follow' might suggest a sort of tagging along with me. Instead, [God's] goodness and mercy are dogged and determined in their pursuit."[2] God has sent them after me.

By now we are very familiar with this psalm showing us how active the shepherd is toward us, and this is another signal that the Lord himself is doing something extraordinary for us.

This sense grows stronger when we consider the two subjects in the pursuit: "goodness" and "mercy." It is no accident that the two are used together here. Neither is an abstract noun that we can understand apart from God, as if the two are ethereal forces out there in the world; rather they are covenantal nouns. In Exodus 33 when the Lord tells Moses that he has found favor in his sight and that he knows Moses by name, Moses asks to see God's glory. In response, God says: "I will make all my goodness pass before you and will proclaim before you my name 'The LORD.' And I will be gracious to whom I will be gracious, and will show mercy on whom I will show mercy" (v. 19). God's glory is revealed as his goodness and his name, and both are expressed in his covenant love to his redeemed people: "The LORD passed before him and proclaimed, 'The LORD, the LORD, a God merciful and gracious, slow to anger, and abounding in steadfast love and faithfulness, keeping steadfast love for thousands, forgiving iniquity and transgression and sin" (Ex. 34:6–7).

In the exodus from Egypt, the people being rescued were pursued by the fury and tyranny of Pharaoh. In their ongoing rescue

2   Briggs, *The Lord Is My Shepherd*, 116.

from sin, they were pursued in the wilderness by the goodness and mercy of their covenant Lord, who did not abandon them in their rebellion but kept making a way for their return to him. David knows that the "goodness" which pursues him is the covenant goodness of God: "You are good and do good" (Ps. 119:68). He knows that the "mercy" hot on his heels is the covenant mercy of God: it is *hesed*, the word for God's steadfast love (as the ESV footnote records). This is his loving-kindness, his loyal, committed, faithful love. With this word, "the relational nature of the term cannot be overemphasized. It describes the duties, benefits, and commitments that one party bears to another party as a result of the relationship between them."[3] Peter Craigie says, "In a sense, the language of Exodus and wilderness which permeates the entire psalm comes to a head in the expression *lovingkindness*; the God of covenant, who in the past had expressed his lovingkindness to his people so bountifully in their redemption, would continue to do so in the future."[4]

One of my favorite films is *The Fugitive*. Harrison Ford plays Dr. Richard Kimble, a man wrongly accused and sentenced to imprisonment for murdering his wife. Kimble escapes from custody and ends up on the run, determined to prove his innocence and clear his name. All the way through, he is hunted down by Tommy Lee Jones's character, Samuel Gerard, a ruthless and determined police officer.

---

3 Nancy de Claissé-Walford, Rolf A. Jacobson, and Beth LaNeel Tanner, *The Book of Psalms*, The New International Commentary on the Old Testament (Grand Rapids, MI: Eerdmans, 2014), 7–8; cited in Briggs, *The Lord Is My Shepherd*, 114.
4 Peter C. Craigie, *Psalms 1–50*, Word Biblical Commentary (Grand Rapids, MI: Zondervan, 2004), 208.

At the very end of the film (spoiler alert), in the showdown, there is a moment when Gerard shouts across the room to where Kimble is hiding: "I believe you—I know you didn't kill your wife."

In that moment, we see the relief wash over Kimble's face. All his efforts have come good; he is vindicated and in the clear. Why? Because, as it turns out, the man who has been pursuing him is good. Kimble is being pursued not by a crooked cop but by a good one, a man capable of showing mercy to those in need. It changes everything.

When we see it or experience it personally, human goodness can be truly amazing. It can be life-giving and liberating.

So, too, steadfast love. In January 2022, Ron and Joyce Bond from Milton Keynes, England, were in the news for being Britain's longest-married couple. That month they were celebrating eighty-one years of married life together. They were 102 and 100 years old respectively. What made me smile the most as I read the story was their recounting how some people said on their wedding day that it would never last! I looked at pictures of them from that day and then looked at them on their eighty-first wedding anniversary, and I realized that what I was looking at was steadfast love. It was love that hadn't gone anywhere other than after the other person. It was love that stayed and sought and stuck.

In Psalm 23 the words of verse 6 tell the most beautiful story. After all the focus on *our* following the good shepherd, we now look over our shoulder and see two things following *us*: goodness and steadfast love. This is God's married love with which he pursues and woos his people. Such pursuit is delightful and honoring to the one so pursued.

It is common for preachers to envisage here "goodness" and "mercy" as being like two sheepdogs of the modern-day shepherd, dispatched by him to bring up the flock from the rear. Spurgeon imagines "great guardian angels" who "will always be with me at my back and my beck."[5] Dale Ralph Davis regards them as "two special agents" and "beloved denizens" whose attempts to overtake and waylay and dog David are a source of immense comfort to him.[6]

As powerful as all these images are, I think the text means to communicate something even more wonderful: these words are another way of saying that the Lord *himself* is pursuing us. They are his divine attributes, yes, but the fact that they are functioning as the joint subject of the verb points to their personification as a way of stressing that these words reveal the covenant Lord himself to us. In the same way that the words "Send out your light and truth; / let them lead me" (Ps. 43:3) is the psalmist's way of asking God himself to lead him to his holy dwelling, so it is here. For God is his own attributes. God doesn't have goodness or love that he might dispatch them; he *is* goodness and love. God sends these attributes after us as a way of giving us himself. "My presence will go with you, and I will give you rest" (Ex. 33:14). So when we put the beauty of these nouns and the intensiveness of the verb together with the sense that God sets out deliberately to have us experience him in our lives through his goodness and his steadfast love, the combined effect is the beautiful reality that it is the Lord himself who pursues his people.

---

5   Charles Spurgeon, *The Treasury of David*, 3 vols. (Peabody, MA: Hendrickson, 1988), 1:356.

6   Dale Ralph Davis, *Slogging Along in the Paths of Righteousness: Psalms 13–24* (Fearn, Ross-shire, Scotland: Christian Focus, 2014), 171.

We are in the final verse of Psalm 23, reading its closing lines. It is lovely to observe that (if we include the title) the third word of the psalm in Hebrew is "LORD" (v. 1) and the third-last word is "LORD" again (v. 6), the only two times the divine name is used in the psalm. This means that the covenant Lord literarily encompasses this whole song even as it praises the covenant Lord for literally encompassing our whole life.[7] The form of the text beautifully matches the content of the text. In verses 1–3 the shepherd is ahead of us, leading us; in verse 4 he is with us, escorting us through the wilderness and then hosting us in his presence (v. 5); and now in verse 6 he is behind us sending his goodness and love to catch us up from behind.

I'm sure you have seen a police escort of an important dignitary where some armored vehicles go ahead and some follow, with the special person in the middle, and there are usually police escorts on either side as well. Is there any safer way to travel? Complete security, perfect protection, full provision: ahead and beside and behind. The sense of Psalm 23 is exactly the same as Psalm 139:

> You hem me in, behind and before,
>   and lay your hand upon me. (v. 5)

But now see something else that elevates these words to a stunning vista. Notice the modifier that begins the verse: "Surely."

---

7   This point is from my brother Jonathan Gibson, "The King of Love My Shepherd Is," a sermon on Ps. 23 preached in the chapel of Westminster Theological Seminary, April 6, 2022, https://www.youtube.com/.

Briggs is right to say of this translation that "there is a hint of gathering up the earlier lines of the poem"[8] so that it is a way of summarizing the effects that will certainly follow in the wake of the Lord's shepherding and hosting. "Surely" is an intensive, affirmative word: this will definitely happen.

But I wonder if this penetrates deeply enough to the profundity of what David is claiming about this shepherd's care. The same word can, in fact, be rendered "only" (as the ESV footnote recognizes). Translated like this, it has a restrictive sense (which necessarily includes the intensive sense) but goes beyond it and says more.

The meaning is that David is looking back over his shoulder at all that has gone before, and he is able to confess that he can see the goodness and the steadfast love of God in every single circumstance of life, the valley of the shadow of death as much as the green pastures and still waters. "In all that happens to me," David is basically saying, "I see *only* his goodness and loving-kindness." As commentators who offer this translation recognize, quite simply, "The expression is remarkable."[9] It is an astonishing confession of faith that the changing scenes of life, which are full of evil, pain, and suffering, never indicate a bad God. Rather, in all that happens—despite all that happens—those who are led by the shepherd and walk with the shepherd all the days of their lives can see that God is only ever good and only ever loving to his sheep all the time. In Davis's

8 Briggs, *The Lord Is My Shepherd*, 113.

9 C. F. Keil and F. Delitzsch, *Commentary on the Old Testament*, vol. 5, *Psalms* (Peabody, MA: Hendrickson, 1996), 209; Dale Ralph Davis provides the same translation in *Slogging Along in the Paths*, 171.

words, "There is a certain chemistry in believing faith that can combine brute facts with buoyant faith."[10]

Just pause to feel the intensity of this. The intensity is not just in the circle it draws around all that happens but so too in the line it draws through all that happens: the Lord is "only" like this "all the days of my life" (Ps. 23:6). Every. Single. Day. Always. He has no off days and no half-hearted days. No days where instead of pursuit he dawdles in his goodness or forgets to follow in his mercy. No days where he drops the ball and sends badness and hatred instead of goodness and love. "You are good and do good" (Ps. 119:68).

If you have ever had a heated argument with a close family member, then you have heard yourself say, or heard it said, "You *always* do such and such." It is usually a telltale sign that all sense of proportion and balance has been lost in the heat of the moment. Such language indicates we would do well to retreat to calm down and regain perspective!

"You are forever doing this . . . you are always doing that . . . *always.*"

But, dear friend reading this, can you see what David is saying? He is using this kind of language about God, but in reverse. It is intense, it is personal, it is so direct in telling God what he always does, but it is the reverse of a heated outburst. Instead, it is a love song: "You, Lord, you *always* do this: you are always good to me, you are always only ever merciful to me. I've blown it so many times, and yet every single time I turn around, I only ever see your goodness and loving-kindness in close pursuit."

---

10 Davis, *Slogging Along in the Paths*, 171.

Isn't this amazing? Imagine just for a moment saying to someone not "you always get it wrong" but, instead, "you always get it right." What kind of person must someone be for that to be true? "You always do no wrong, you never commit injustice, you are always merciful, you are always faithful, always compassionate, always forgiving, always kind." It is so beautiful. Human steadfast love, eighty-one years of love, can be amazing. But can you take in being pursued by God himself, by the goodness of the Lord of the burning bush, by the steadfast love of the Lord Jesus our good shepherd? There is only ever goodness and mercy because this is who God is himself.

(This, by the way, is a lesson for us shepherds. When we wield the rod or extend the staff and pull the sheep back, as the sheep look back over their shoulders, they need to see goodness and mercy in how we have led them. Many shepherds wonder why the sheep bristle at our pastoral attention, but maybe they feel pursued more by the under-shepherd's exasperation than by the chief shepherd's loving-kindness.)

Yet we must reckon with the staggering implications of this word "only." Can it really be true that there is "only" goodness and steadfast love following me. Really? In my life, and in yours, I'm sure, it often looks like there are plenty of things that are not good and not loving, and those things seem to be winning.

Is it possible to believe this "only" and to live with this hope?

I tremble as I write these lines, and some of us will tremble to read them. Maybe right now you are in the realm of raw, brutal realities that have ravaged your life, and it seems impossible beyond belief that you might ever combine these with "buoyant faith." Death. Illness. Injury. Infertility. Grief. You are right there in the valley of the shadow of death. Darkness seems your closest friend, your only friend; bewilderment and perplexity pursue you. Goodness and mercy are nowhere to be seen, never mind the "only" things to be seen.

Let me say, as we wrestle with this theology, that if your own current experience cannot handle this perspective, just take time to note the vantage point of the guest here in verse 6: goodness and mercy are pursuing him. He is moving forward, and they are *behind* him. Sometimes, only when we look back on events will we ever be able to see the goodness and steadfast love of the Lord in them. If you cannot feel it now, the Lord is still with you in the valley. He will still walk with you without fail all your days, and one day it may be that you look back on the worst of experiences, the most dreadful of times, the deepest of dark valleys, and you will be able say, "I see it now: God's goodness and God's mercy never left me, even then."

Many commentators helpfully suggest that David's own experience teaches us this. A sordid affair, incest, murder, civil war, and the death of his children—we should not underestimate the lived wilderness experience of the ordinary man who penned this psalm. "Perhaps some of the good was behind him, protecting him, but he chose to turn aside from it. Yet as he looked back he could vividly remember the good that followed him."[11]

Lived experience does not have to be the only lens for our circumstances. It is also possible in the life of faith to come to a lived

11 Kenneth E. Bailey, *The Good Shepherd: A Thousand-Year Journey from Psalm 23 to the New Testament* (London: SPCK, 2015), 61.

conviction "that for those who love God all things work together for good" (Rom. 8:28). This conviction does not erase the pain in the moment, but it can anchor it and provide a compass point in the valley as we lift up our pain to God. Dale Ralph Davis illustrates the truth of Psalm 23:6 like this:

> In the summer of 1680, Alan Cameron, the Covenanter, was in prison in Edinburgh and did not know that his son Richard had been killed in battle at Airds Moss. A trooper opened the door and flung down a bloodied head and two hands, and yelled, "Do you know whose these are?" Cameron took the gory tokens upon his knees and held them. "Yes," he said, "they are my son's, my dear son's." And then he went on: "Good is the Lord, who could never wrong me or mine, and has made goodness and mercy to follow me all the days of my life." It may stretch our minds, but valleys (v. 4) and enemies (v. 5) and apparently body parts do not negate the truth of verse 6a.[12]

There are examples of this in nearer times as well. Dr. Helen Roseveare was a British medical missionary in the Belgian Congo with the Heart of Africa Mission in the 1950s and 1960s. In 1964, in the midst of a Congolese civil war, she was brutally beaten and raped. "On that dreadful night, beaten and bruised, terrified and tormented, unutterably alone, I had felt at last God had failed me. Surely He could have stepped in earlier, surely things need not have gone that far. I had

---

12 Davis, *Slogging Along in the Paths*, 171.

reached what seemed to be the ultimate depth of despairing nothingness."[13] These are words anyone could surely identify with in such trauma.

And yet her lived experience also became shaped by living conviction too:

Through the brutal heartbreaking experience of rape, God met with me—with outstretched arms of love. It was an unbelievable experience: He was so utterly there, so totally understanding, his comfort was so complete—and suddenly I knew—I really knew that his love was unutterably sufficient. He did love me! He did understand![14]

Does it not seem impossible to us that in an occasion such as this God might be pursuing one of his sheep? But it is evident if you read Roseveare's life story that her sense of what God is seeking in a person, and what he wants to do with and through that person, is so much deeper and so much more profound than we often settle for ourselves.

One word became unbelievably clear, and that word was privilege. He didn't take away pain or cruelty or humiliation. No! It was all there, but now it was altogether different. It was with him, for him, in him. He was actually offering me the inestimable privilege of sharing in some little way the edge of the fellowship of his suffering. In the weeks of imprison-

13 Justin Taylor, "A Woman of Whom the World Was Not Worthy: Helen Roseveare (1925–2016)," TGC (blog), December 7, 2016, https://www.thegospelcoalition.org/.
14 Taylor, "A Woman of Whom the World Was Not Worthy."

ment that followed and in the subsequent years of continued service, looking back, one has tried to "count the cost," but I find it all swallowed up in privilege. The cost suddenly seems very small and transient in the greatness and permanence of the privilege.[15]

I do not share this story to suggest that each of our valleys will always lead to exactly the same encounter with God as Helen Roseveare experienced. But I do want to suggest that she is part of a chorus of faithful witnesses—stretching all the way back through church history, into the pages of Scripture to King David, and back beyond him in the storyline of redemption—who proclaim to us in our pain that the shepherd has not abandoned us. Each one teaches us that God is working out his sovereign purposes for our lives perfectly in keeping with who he is as the great "I am," our Lord of covenant faithfulness.

This is the story of the Bible. Jacob, one of Scripture's scoundrels, who knew such pain and heartache in his own life through his own sin and the sins of others, still confesses at the end: God "has been my shepherd all my life long to this day" (Gen. 48:15). It is remarkable that the first reference to God as shepherd in the Bible is personal before it is corporate. Think of Joseph, Moses, Hannah, Naomi, Ruth, and David, to name just a few in redemption's great story. Ask believers who have been through the darkest valley, the fiery furnace, the deep waters—ask them

---

15 Taylor, "A Woman of Whom the World Was Not Worthy." Dr. Helen Roseveare's autobiography is available in two volumes, *Give Me This Mountain* (Fearn, Ross-shire, Scotland: Christian Focus, 2012) and *He Gave Us a Valley* (Fearn, Ross-shire, Scotland: Christian Focus, 2013).

what it was like, and they will each say to you, "The LORD was with me."[16]

The Lord is with you.

At the funeral of my niece, Leila Judith Grace, who arrived into the world stillborn, we sang a glorious hymn that some attribute to John Calvin, "I Greet Thee, Who My Sure Redeemer Art." It contains this beautiful verse:

Thou hast the true and perfect gentleness,
no harshness hast thou and no bitterness:
make us to taste the sweet grace found in thee
and ever stay in thy sweet unity.[17]

As my brother and his wife have often mentioned since Leila's death, sometimes these things are best contemplated by reverent, patient silence as we acknowledge that the shepherd's true and perfect gentleness is pursuing us by a sore providence. Sometimes, with Job, we need to learn to cover our mouths and to wait on God, lest we accuse the shepherd of bitter harshness toward his sheep.

Sometimes these things are best sung through tears and sung by faith in the night, not by sight.

But each time the confession of faith is the same: the Lord is good, and he is only ever good. And in all his ways with all his people he only ever sends goodness and mercy.

16 Gibson, "The King of Love My Shepherd Is."
17 https:// hymnary.org/.

9

Where He Invites

I AM WRITING THESE WORDS from a remote location in the Scottish Highlands where I have stowed away on a writing retreat. The scenery is stunning, the accommodation is beautiful, and the provision that has been made for me is more generous than I could have envisaged. I have all that I need.

And yet I want to go home.

Several days have passed, and as much as there has been enjoyment of the new surroundings and the pleasure of new acquaintances, I am not with the people I love most in the place I hold dear.

I am not home.

If it is true that "you are with me" (Ps. 23:4) is the heart of the whole Bible in a nutshell, then it is also true that in the closing words of Psalm 23 we have the climax of the Bible's whole storyline expressed in a final, beautiful confession of faith:

I shall dwell in the house of the LORD
    forever. (v. 6)

This is the ultimate "being with." This is the drama of the Scriptures, and it is the personal invitation of our shepherd-host: he comes to be with us (v. 4) so that we can go and be with him (v. 6). He invites us to dwell with him where he dwells and to be there with him forever. As Richard Briggs says so nicely, here now, at last, "the psalm arrives at an assurance that transcends the immediate imagery of the poem."[1]

I have occasionally been in beautiful homes with generous hosts, or nice hotels where I experience refreshing treatment as a guest. But always the day comes when I have to leave. The hotel has lovely food and pleasant rooms, but the reality is that establishment treats me well because I treat it well with money. Stop the money and the welcome would be abruptly withdrawn. I am treated well because I'm paying for it, not because I am loved. Even in the nice home of the generous host, we are friends, yes, but we are not family. I am only visiting there; I do not live there.

In Psalm 23:6 David takes us from all our days of pressing onward with the shepherd in front of us and from all our days of looking back over his goodness and mercy behind us. We have been hemmed in safely all along the paths and in the valleys, but now he asserts with bold confidence that we are going to make it all the way to the shepherd's house. And as we enter we will hear: "You're with me now. You're home. Welcome. This is it. Hang your hat. This is where you shall live forever."

There is some debate as to the meaning of the phrase "forever" in the verse. It literally means "for length of days," and so some question the sense of endless duration, the idea of an afterlife.

---

1 Richard S. Briggs, *The Lord Is My Shepherd: Psalm 23 for the Life of the Church* (Grand Rapids, MI: Baker Academic, 2021), 124.

Maybe David is simply saying this is where he will be for as long as he lives. But I think it is best to read "length of days" not merely as synonymous with "all the days of my life" in the preceding line but as intensifying that duration. In Psalms 21:4 and 93:5 and Lamentations 5:20, the phrase "length of days" is clearly used with the sense of "forevermore" in ways that we associate with unending life. Many commentators make compelling cases for why that appears to be in view here.[2] When we live with the Lord, we will never have to move out. It will never end.

I want to beg your indulgence one final time in this shortest of the chapters to consider the other footnote in the verse and to see the riches it lays out before us. You will see that our closing line could be rendered "and I shall *return to dwell* in the house of the LORD forever." There is very good reason for this translation, and I want to commend it to you as we come to finish this book together. For it manages in a few words to capture both the Bible story and that sense I described a few lines above about how my current location is not home. Why do I have this longing for a particular place?

Human beings are walking, talking homing devices. Our built-in satellite navigation systems are hardwired to people and place, and to particular people and specific places to which we seek to return. Where does this come from, and why can this desire be so intense?

I believe it is how God made us. We were created for fellowship with God; the whole point of our existence is to dwell with him.

---

2 So Dale Ralph Davis, *Slogging Along in the Paths of Righteousness: Psalms 13–24* (Fearn, Ross-shire, Scotland: Christian Focus, 2014), 172; and see especially Briggs, *The Lord Is My Shepherd*, 125–27.

This fellowship—as we know all too well—has been fractured by the fall and the waywardness of our rebellion and sin, but none of these calamities have succeeded in erasing the original design. Our GPS is now faulty; we do not know the way back to God by ourselves, and we do not always want to find him—in fact, often quite the opposite—yet none of it removes our deep innate need to relate to our Creator. As Augustine famously said, "You move us to delight in praising You; for You have made us for Yourself, and our hearts are restless until they rest in You."[3]

This is a confession of faith about return. It is a recognition that human beings belong with the one who made them, wherever else we belong. I think it's why every sense of belonging is an echo from the deep heart-sonar signals for our true eternal home. And Psalm 23 is a song of praise to the God who has come to get us and bring us home. The journey is long, so we need a shepherd; it is dangerous, so we need a companion; and it is wearisome, so we need a host. But the journey has always had an ultimate destination in mind: the restoration of return to the house of the Lord.

I discovered in writing this book that my favorite song version of Psalm 23, which is printed after this chapter—"The King of Love My Shepherd Is"—contains a verse we should think quite unusual if we only follow the standard English translations of the psalm. Have you ever noticed this before?

Perverse and foolish I have strayed,
but in his love he sought me;

---

3 Augustine, *Confessions* 1.1.1, New Advent, https://www.newadvent.org/.

and on his shoulder gently laid,
and home, rejoicing, brought me.[4]

Scholars such as Kenneth Bailey point out that, in fact, this is a beautiful rendering of what many regard as the best translation of Psalm 23:2, which we took to be "He restores my soul." A literal rendering of the word for "restore" could, however, offer this meaning: "He causes my soul to return." Bailey makes a most persuasive case that the best sense of verses 1–3 is that the sheep has actually wandered from the right paths, and the shepherd's close work here is to personally find and fetch and return the sheep to where it properly belongs. The sense could even be "He causes my soul to repent." As W. S. Plumer says, "Restoration from wandering seems to have been by far the most common idea attached to this clause."[5] The picture is so beautiful: the sheep is wayward, but the shepherd is watchful. We are prone to wander, but he is poised to watch and to retrieve when we do so.[6]

Viewing it this way, we can see how deeply Psalm 23 connects with the story of the good shepherd in Luke 15:1–7, and the subsequent stories of a lost coin (Luke 15:8–10) and two lost sons (Luke 15:11–32). Jesus has come to seek and to save the lost, to find the missing, and to return the wayward to repentant restoration. This is the story of the Bible. It is the gospel: that God so

---

4   H. W. Baker, rev. The Jubilate Group © 1982 The Jubilate Group (Admin. Hope Publishing Company, www.hopepublishing.com). All rights reserved. Used by permission.

5   William S. Plumer, *Psalms: A Critical and Expository Commentary with Doctrinal and Practical Remarks* (Edinburgh: Banner of Truth, 1975), 311.

6   Jonathan Gibson, "The King of Love My Shepherd Is," a sermon on Ps. 23 preached in the chapel of Westminster Theological Seminary, April 6, 2022, https://www.youtube .com/.

loved the world that he sent his Son to shepherd the lost sheep of Israel (Matt. 15:24) and, more than that, to call others not of that flock to come and enter his fold (John 10:16; 17:20–26).

Think again about that shepherd boy who died alone in the blizzard in the Scottish highlands. Yes, he was lost—but Jesus found him. The good shepherd came to him that night and picked him up and took him home.[7] If you have lost loved ones in Christ to the shroud of death, you need to know they are not lost to Jesus. He knows where they are and how to find them. He will come and get them and bring them home. If those you love in Christ have fallen, he will pick them up and on his shoulder gently lay them. He will cause all his lost sheep to return. We should never forget that the shepherd we belong to is the Lord of the burning bush, whose undimming strength comes from his self-existence and the extent of his unending care from his self-sufficiency. He is not capable of losing any of his sheep from his fold. He has conquered our greatest enemies of sin and death by entering the valley of the shadow of death, being forsaken by his Father, and having only the cup of cursing to drink, not the cup of blessing. On the cross he thirsted; his cup did not overflow. And yet, having endured death, he emerged on the other side, victoriously alive, and now he is leading his people home. "In my Father's house are many rooms. . . . And if I go and prepare a place for you, I will come again and will take you to myself, that where I am you may be also" (John 14:2–3).

This means, then, that this beautiful psalm is not just the story of a sheep's daily journey, out of the fold in the morning, doing

---

7   Gibson, "The King of Love My Shepherd Is."

its thing in the pastures and the valleys, and then returning safely home again with the shepherd at dusk. It is the story, ultimately, of how ever since our first parents' fall in Eden, we were exiled from the garden, the dwelling place of the Lord, so that God's people were in need of an exodus salvation to take us from the land of sin and slavery to the land of promise. In that land, however, we replayed our rebellion and not only vandalized a perfect garden but, this time, ruined a land flowing with milk and honey; and so the pattern continued. Exiled once more into slavery, God's people needed a new exodus salvation to restore us to the promised land. It is true that a return from exile brought deliverance, yes, but it was not complete; it was not total; it did not seem to contain *everything* that the prophets had promised. Ever since the dawn of time we have been longing to return home, and that return is made possible only by the coming of the Lord Jesus, the true good shepherd who arrived to lead us home.

This home to which we are returning is Eden restored; but more than this, it is also Eden recalibrated to cosmic proportions.

Eden was the first dwelling place on earth of God with us. It was the first house where God and man lived together in perfect fellowship. Ever since, every dwelling place of God on earth has been patterned on Eden: the tabernacle and then the temple were built as garden-sanctuaries with walls decorated with Edenic images of trees and flowers and precious stones. The tabernacle and temple had within them the ultimate dwelling place, "the holy of holies" (or "Most Holy Place," ESV), but astonishingly, at the end, in the book of Revelation, a "holy of holies" is not to be found. It is absent in Revelation's glorious vision of God's end-time dwelling. The reason for this is simply stunning: the holy of holies—a perfect cube whose floor, walls, and ceiling were made of gold—has now expanded to fill the entire new earth as a city made of "pure gold" (Rev. 21:18) and measured as square in its dimensions. Eden's gold, reused in the most holy places of the tabernacle and temple, has now filled the whole earth to tell the gospel story that "God's special presence, formerly limited to the holy of holies, has now burst forth to encompass the whole earth."[8] This is why the holy city, the new Jerusalem, comes down from heaven to be the place where God will dwell with us: "Behold, the dwelling place of God is with man. He will dwell with them, and they will be his people, and God himself will be with them as their God" (Rev. 21:3).

This is the house of the Lord.

We have a longing for this kind of glorious house and this kind of joyful homecoming reunion at a very profound level, I think, because we know what it is to live among the ruins in this world. Simple homes can be the happiest palaces on earth if filled with love and life, or they can be the most awful dungeons when overrun with strife or sorrow. Psalm 23 resonates with us so deeply because it speaks to this yearning for all to be well and to arrive, at last, in a place of unreserved welcome and untainted beauty and perfection. So we live with Christ our shepherd amid the tension of life, the now and the not-yet of his perfect rule. For now, we are not home, but we are heading there because he is leading us.

George MacDonald wrote these beautiful words to Lady Mount-Temple following the death of her husband in 1888:

8   G. K. Beale, *The Temple and the Church's Mission: A Biblical Theology of the Dwelling Place of God* (Nottingham: Inter-Varsity Press, 2004), 370.

We are in a house with windows on all sides. On one side the sweet garden is trampled and torn, the beeches blown down, the fountain broken; you sit and look out, and it is all very miserable. Shut the window. I do not mean forget the garden as it was, but do not brood on it as it is. Open the window on the other side, where the great mountains shoot heavenward, and the stars rising and setting, crown their peaks. Down those stairs look for the descending feet of the Son of Man coming to comfort you. This world, if it were alone, would not be worth much—I should be miserable already; but it is the porch to the Father's home, and he does not expect us to be quite happy, and knows we must sometimes be very unhappy till we get there: we are getting nearer.[9]

You are not journeying just somewhere with your shepherd. Your exodus journey is not an aimless wandering in the wilderness. You are on your Father's porch.

You are journeying to the house of the Lord.

You are heading home.

Bring us, O Lord God, at our last awakening into the house and gate of heaven, to enter into that gate and dwell in that house, where there shall be no darkness nor dazzling, but one equal light; no noise nor silence, but one equal music; no fears nor hopes, but one equal possession; no ends nor beginnings,

---

9   Cited in Glenn Edward Sadler, "Defining Death as 'More Life': Unpublished Letters by George MacDonald," *North Wind: A Journal of George MacDonald Studies* 3 (1984): 13–14.

but one equal eternity; in the habitations of thy glory and dominion, world without end.[10]

———

The King of love my shepherd is,
whose goodness fails me never;
I nothing lack if I am his
and he is mine for ever.

Where streams of living waters flow,
a ransomed soul, he leads me;
and where the richest pastures grow,
with food from heaven feeds me.

Perverse and foolish I have strayed,
but in his love he sought me;
and on his shoulder gently laid,
and home, rejoicing, brought me.

In death's dark vale I fear no ill
with you, dear LORD, beside me;
your rod and staff my comfort still,
your cross before to guide me.

---

10 From *Daily Prayer*, ed. Eric Milner-White and G. W. Briggs (Harmondsworth, UK: Penguin, 1959), http://assets.newscriptorium.com/collects-and-prayers/daily_prayer .htm; building on the words of John Donne, sermon 146, on Acts 7:60, preached at Whitehall, February 29, 1627.

You spread a banquet in my sight
of grace beyond all knowing;
and O, the wonder and delight
from your pure chalice flowing!

And so through all the length of days
your goodness fails me never:
Good Shepherd, may I sing your praise
within your house for ever!

H. W. BAKER, REV. THE JUBILATE GROUP

Acknowledgments

MY GREATEST DEBT ON EARTH is to the two families that encircle my life. There is the family of my wife, Angela, with my children, Archie, Ella, Sam, and Lily, and my parents, who do so much for us. And there is the family of Trinity Church, Aberdeen. My first family makes writing possible; my second family makes writing pleasurable. The Trinity family's encouragement as this material was first presented to them in sermon form spurred me on to write it up in book form.

I was greatly helped by a sermon on Psalm 23 preached by my brother Jonathan when he was a minister at Cambridge Presbyterian Church. Some of his insights are used here, and I am particularly indebted to him for help with the Hebrew of the psalm. Jonathan subsequently preached on Psalm 23 again after I did, and we have freely shared quotes, illustrations, and our developing understanding of the text together to the point where, in places, we cannot now remember who saw or said something first—except where, if it was really good, it was obviously from me. Nevertheless, I have sought to credit his material at every point where appropriate.

Hannah McEwan added "research assistant" to the already variegated role of being a ministry trainee at Trinity, and proved to be an enormous help with both materials and excellent feedback. Special thanks are due to the MacKenzie family for the kindness of five fruitful days in "The Writer's Loft" at Geanies House in beautiful Fearn, Ross-shire.

It is a delight to dedicate this book to Drew Tulloch, a mainstay of Trinity life in his role as our music coordinator. For more than four decades now Drew's musical gifts, coupled with his spiritual sensitivity and personal selflessness, have served the people of God in Aberdeen to our immense delight and benefit. The congregations of St Devenick's Church, Gilcomston South Church, High Church Hilton, and Trinity have been immeasurably blessed, successively, by Drew's enrichment of corporate worship with excellent music and his care and mentoring of other musicians and hymn writers. I have valued his godliness, friendship, and wisdom more than I can say.

One of my prayers for Drew echoes that of John Stott's study assistant who signed off a letter to "Uncle John" with the words: "Please live forever." Drew, doubtless, will be the first to say he hopes the Lord does not answer that prayer in the way that I wish! So—in lieu of an unlikely answer to prayer—this book is dedicated to him with heartfelt thanks, and with my prayers for him and Fiona, along with their son, David, that the close presence of the shepherd and the continual refreshment of Psalm 23 would be their portion through all the length of days.

General Index

Scripture Index